INTO THE GARDEN
WITH CHARLES

INTO THE GARDEN WITH CHARLES

A Memoir

Clyde Phillip Wachsberger

WITH WATERCOLORS BY THE AUTHOR

Farrar, Straus and Giroux   New York

Farrar, Straus and Giroux
18 West 18th Street, New York 10011

Text and watercolors copyright © 2012 by Charles Randall Dean
All rights reserved
Distributed in Canada by D&M Publishers, Inc.
Printed in China
Originally published in 2010, in somewhat different form, in a limited
edition printed by the Studley Press, Dalton, Massachusetts
First Farrar, Straus and Giroux edition, 2012

Library of Congress Cataloging-in-Publication Data
Wachsberger, Clyde.
    Into the garden with Charles : a memoir / Clyde Phillip Wachsberger ;
with Watercolors by the Author.
        p.   cm.
    ISBN 978-0-374-17571-9 (alk. paper)
    1. Wachsberger, Clyde.   2. Gay men—New York (State)—Biography.
3. Gay couples—New York (State)—Biography.   I. Title.

HQ75.8.W33 A3 2012
306.76'62092274725—dc23
[B]

                                                              2011024869

Designed by Jonathan D. Lippincott

www.fsgbooks.com

1   3   5   7   9   10   8   6   4   2

For my mother,
Helen Dreher Wachsberger,
and for Charles's mother,
Evelyn Barker Dean

Contents

Illustrations

INTO THE GARDEN
WITH CHARLES

Every garden tells a story.
Ours tells a love story.

The Privet Hedge

Charles is on the next-to-top step of our wobbly A-frame ladder, trimming our privet hedge, wielding the electric clippers with the concentration of a sculptor. I'm on the bottom rung, steadying him, looking up at him tall against puffy white clouds and brilliant blue sky. He's wearing an old striped pullover torn here and there by rose thorns, faded pants that were once dress slacks, and muck boots that were a Christmas present from his mother a few years ago. His cap has a flap to protect his neck from the sun. It reminds me of a French Foreign Legionnaire's hat.

Not for the first time, I wonder if I have invented Charles. For half a century I daydreamed of a devoted companion, a best friend, a cherished lover. Maybe I'm still dreaming. If any neighbors strolled past right now, would they see me holding on to an empty ladder, staring up at the sky, talking to myself?

The clippers stop snarling. The ladder shudders. Charles is moving up to the top step. I snap out of my reverie to warn, "There's a notice glued on that step that says you shouldn't stand on it."

"Please give me the small pruners."

Without looking, he reaches an empty hand toward me. He wiggles his fingers, so I place the pruners in his hand.

Charles is six foot four, but just now he needs the top of the ladder to get at a wayward sprig interrupting the flawlessly rounded surface he has shaped. He stretches forward over the smooth curve of the hedge, one long leg far out for balance, snips what he wants to get rid of, brushes away the few bits of leaves with a flourish, hands me the pruners without looking. From his back pocket he pulls out the nail scissors that are usually on a shelf over our bathroom sink and snips off one unruly leaf.

The hedge was a foot tall when I bought this property almost thirty years ago. Now it is trimmed high and billowy like a soft fur collar around the house. There was once a gap in the hedge, but years ago I planted a climbing red rose there with the idea that it would someday cascade over the privet. Friends warned me that it would be a nightmare to prune around a rose. They were right. I never got it looking the way I had imagined. Now Charles has the privet running smoothly, right up to the rose's thorny stems tumbling down the hedge in sprays of garnet blossoms.

I shift my weight to secure the ladder. Next to me is the cucumber magnolia that Charles started from seed years before we met, now taller than our house. Through its lower branches I can just see our new rose arbors. Charles had the idea that they would define entrances into our garden. Opera-velvet red 'Etoile de Hollande' and silvery pink 'Viking Queen' are already draping themselves over the arches.

I notice our friend Karen walking toward us from her home down the block, and at the same time Rover, our Havanese, has seen her from his upstairs window, where he's been watching Charles prune. He's barking to let us know she's coming for a visit, telling us to stop hedging and come play. He wants us all together.

Karen calls out her hellos, Charles answers over the hedge, Rover barks.

Maybe this is all real.

A House on Village Lane

It would be easy to pretend that Village Lane itself is a fantasy, a street conjured in a daydream. That's why I wanted to live there. The entrance to the lane is Y-shaped around a small paved island sporting an obelisk known as the Monument and dedicated to local soldiers lost in the Civil War, although the inscription refers to the War of the Rebellion. The soldiers' family names carved in its stone sides can still be found in the local telephone book. Summertime flower beds surrounding the base are the patriotic red, white, and blue of geranium and petunia and lobelia. A tall flagpole next to the obelisk flies the American flag.

Across the main road from the Monument, in a grassy island bordered with cobblestones, a huge, ancient sycamore looms against the sky. Locally, everyone calls it the Buttonwood Tree. Sycamore wood was once used to make buttons, but not everyone remembers this. A bronze plaque on the tree's patchy trunk claims that it was already growing here when the Declaration of Independence was signed. No one knows for sure if this is true. The old tree is late to leaf out each spring, and until it does there is always concern that it may have finally died, rebutted by the opinion that it should finally be allowed to die. Then it leafs out for another summer. On holidays, two small American flags are wedged behind the corners of the plaque.

These two landmarks figure in directions to Village Lane for anyone coming from Manhattan: turn right at the obelisk across from the big tree. From there, Village Lane runs south through the hamlet of Orient, on the eastern tip of Long Island's northern shore, past clapboard and shingled eighteenth-century houses, mostly white with green or black shutters, and past a few Victorian homes that are thought of as the new ones. Along the way is the Country Store, where you can buy newspapers, canned goods, fresh local eggs, and home-made soup in the winter or ice cream in the summer; next to that is a small post office. Across the lane is a collection of very old buildings set around an open green, which together form the Oysterponds Historical Society, Oysterponds being an earlier name for Orient.

The lane continues south, curving gently, almost touches a sheltered bay, then makes a sharp left turn and becomes King Street, which runs out into farmland.

One rainy December Sunday in 1982, my friend Edwin and I were reading by the wood-burning stove in his Orient living room. Edwin was immersed in *The New York Times*, while I was lost in plant catalogues. Rain rattled the old window-panes. Edwin's house had been built in the early 1700s by a ship's captain who understood weather. It was sound against the elements, standing on its corner lot for almost three hundred years, just behind the Buttonwood Tree.

Edwin and I had met a few years earlier at a summer party in Orient. I was visiting my older sister, Freddie, and her partner, Sylvia, that weekend. Their house was a short

walk beyond the hamlet, and their garden stretched into fields
of wild Queen Anne's lace and goldenrod, perfect for outdoor
parties. Edwin had recently bought his house, and word of a
new single man in town had traveled fast through Orient.
Freddie and Sylvia invited him to their party. This one was a
theme party: a Robigalia, in honor of Robiga, the ancient
Roman goddess of mold. Orient summers are humid. Everyone
complains as everything in the house gets moldy: shoes turn
penicillin green, porch walls grow peppery black spores, and
envelopes seal themselves shut. But none of us would have
heard of Robiga except that Freddie had taught ancient
Roman art. The Robigalia was her idea. It was meant to be a
costume party, but I was the only one who took that seriously.
I wore a vintage black bowler hat, pink boxer shorts, black
dress shoes and socks, and nothing else. The idea was that all
my other clothes had gotten too moldy to wear. I was almost
still young enough to pull it off. I, or my costume, caught
Edwin's eye, and since he didn't know anyone there, I spent
the afternoon talking with him. I envied his excitement
about his new home. He was looking forward to having a
garden but was daunted by the idea of clearing the junk out
of the messy yard. I offered to help.

Edwin and I liked each other and at first tried being a
couple. Orient had that effect on us. It was a community of
couples and families, straight and gay. Our friends were couples. It was easier to fit into the social life there as a couple.
But we were better at being friends than lovers. We got into
the habit of spending most weekends together in Orient.
Edwin let me choose plants for his garden, and sometimes I
ordered plants from catalogues as gifts for him, plants that
I wanted the experience of growing.

I'd not yet had a garden of my own. I grew up in Riverdale, a suburb of Manhattan. We had a front lawn and a back-

yard. I could go play *outside*, I could go into the *yard*, but there wasn't a *garden*. I longed for the storybook gardens illustrated in my children's books from the thirties and forties, books that had been my sister's before becoming mine. In those gardens, magic happened under huge leaves, flowers smiled or frowned like human faces, and little children discovered worlds much more interesting than what they knew at home. These were gardens where adventures began. If a prince appeared in the story, those adventures ended in romance.

I was obsessed with a field of daylilies in our Riverdale neighborhood. These common roadside daylilies amazed me, because in July they were able to change the whole field from green to gold. I would cajole my mother into driving past whenever we were going somewhere. On spring days, on the way home from school, when other parents were taking their kids to Little League or piano lessons or Hebrew school, we'd drive to that open field so I could see how the daylilies' bright leaves were coming along. I wanted to lie down on that carpet of sunlit green, to bury my face in the greenness, but I knew my mother would be embarrassed by such abandon. *What would people think?* she'd have said. Once, in July, when the field was a sea of orange, like a sunset on a calm ocean, I begged my mother to park for a few minutes. She nosed our gray 1950s fishtail Cadillac against that expanse of bright color, where it sat like a beached whale while I opened my door and just stared. Finally, I could not contain my desire. I rushed out of the car to break off armloads of flowering stems for a bouquet to bring home. My mother worried that this might be illegal, like killing a praying mantis, that we'd be caught and maybe arrested. Neither of us knew enough about gardening to realize that no one would mind if we dug up one or two daylily plants, or that if we did and then planted them we'd certainly have our own hundreds of daylilies in a few years. I made do with a hastily stolen bouquet in a vase. But I wanted that field. I wanted those thousands of orange flowers to be mine.

When I was in my twenties, Freddie bought a house in Brewster, New York, that had remnants of an old garden around it, including beds of crowded daylilies. Whenever I visited for a weekend, she gave me garden chores and even let me make some creative decisions. Once I transplanted daylilies onto a shallow ledge high atop a six-foot-tall boulder near her driveway. That was the first time I ever wrenched daylilies out of the ground. The little tubers at the base of the foliage looked like tiny sweet potatoes. I had no idea what I was doing, only an image in my mind of the effect I wanted. There was hardly any room for soil on top of that boulder, and certainly no drainage, but the tough daylilies survived. I loved the pictures they created, bright green swords of foliage sprawling out of that rock high above our heads in spring, dotted with orange flowers in July. Mostly, I loved that they *thrived*, against all odds. Each year they spread, finally filling up the whole pocket in the rock. When Freddie decided to sell her house, I felt sad about the daylilies. I would miss them. But then, if she hadn't moved, I might never have wound up in Orient.

My sister had always opened up new worlds to me. She was ten when I was born, and immediately nicknamed me Skipper, since my parents had named me Clyde for the family doctor who had delivered me. "He can't go through life with that name," she told our parents. Later, Freddie's interest in ancient art and archaeology inspired me to seek out the old, the antique, the unusual. Her nineteenth-century Brewster home had shingles aged to a dark chocolate color, and small rooms with rustic plaster walls and exposed beams. She had painted the corner beams of the bedroom I stayed in a lustrous khaki green. I loved the way those beams' irregular shiny edges met the matte white walls, as if they had grown together over generations and conformed to each other's needs. There was an old wooden bed and side table, and a few well-worn but fascinating objects that Freddie had collected from here and there on her travels. Whenever I visited, I daydreamed about having a house just like it, surrounded by banks of my own daylilies.

I was thrilled to find masses of old roadside daylilies around Edwin's house in Orient. They inspired me to line his driveway with them. We separated the clumps and replanted them, then lugged interesting rocks up from the beach— small versions of the Brewster boulder—to place randomly among them. I wanted the effect of a very old bed that had grown around the rocks. In fact, it achieved that look its first summer.

That rainy December day in Edwin's living room, as I looked longingly through one mail-order plant catalogue after another, I was aware that the garden at Edwin's house wasn't really mine. It was not even *ours*. It was Edwin's, and he planned on renting his house for the summer while he traveled. Whatever I had already planted might grow lush and leafy without my ever seeing it. I'd miss the daylily bloom. That made me sad.

Edwin tapped the page of his newspaper. I looked up from the photos of plants I might never order.

"Skip, I think this is that house you like so much. The one on Village Lane. It's for sale."

He meant the little white-shingled house I passed every time I walked from his house to Freddie's. It seemed abandoned and lonely, and my heart always went out to it.

"I don't have the money to buy a house."

I was working as a scenic artist, collecting unemploy-

It seemed abandoned and lonely, and my heart always went out to it.

ment checks between jobs, and, with a friend, I had recently started Tromploy, Inc., a trompe l'oeil and mural painting company in Manhattan, which wasn't getting many clients.

"Let's just go and look at it. It's a perfect diversion for a rainy afternoon," Edwin said.

We both loved old houses that had interesting histories. Edwin called the real estate agent, who said he'd meet us there in half an hour.

"I think there's something about the house in this book of historic Orient," Edwin said, already leafing through a slender paperbound book that he kept in a pile of magazines next to his rocking chair. "Here!" He indicated a grainy black-and-white photograph.

"All evidence points to this as being one of the very oldest houses in the village," the accompanying text began. There was mention of the framing being secured by pegs because the wood was too hard for nails, of wide floorboards, and of a wooden sink in one room. The house had sold in 1871 for $550.

We got on our slickers and grabbed umbrellas.

Just outside Edwin's yard, the ancient Buttonwood Tree scratched at the gray sky. In the summer, the pavement was always dry under its enormous leafy canopy even in a downpour, but that day the bare branches offered no protection.

We hurried across the Main Road, past the Monument, its flower beds bare and muddy. Rain glazed the names of the lost soldiers. The tall flagpole held a drenched American flag.

The house we were going to see stood close to the lane. Because there was no sidewalk on that side, I was used to looking at it from across the street. The front was plain, with four tall windows and a wooden door on the right. There were two eyebrow windows above, but the house didn't seem tall enough to have a second story. The rows of shingles sagged out of line. There didn't appear to be any true square angles.

A privet hedge clipped as short as an edging in a knot garden bordered the front of the house. I saw no purpose for it except to define a line between the house and the road. The hedge had two gaps: one at the front door, which made sense, and one opposite the last window at the other end, which made no sense.

"Skip, I bet the original door to the house was here!" Edwin pointed to the window behind the gap. "See, there's this wonderful old stepping-stone by the foundation." With his foot, he scraped away overgrown grass to expose the stone. "That's why there's an opening through the hedge here. Where the door is at the other end must be a later addition."

Now it made sense. Edwin had learned a lot about old houses from fixing up his own.

I imagined the hedge grown tall and dense. I might plant a climbing rose in the useless gap, so that it would spill over the hedge in a wild cottage-garden abandon, as if it had been growing there for generations. I would have to find out which rose would be best for such an effect.

We walked up a short driveway past two old lichen-covered apple trees to a shingled garage crammed with storm doors, odd-shaped windows, broken furniture, and piles of wood. I noticed a barrel of long-handled garden tools, hoes and rakes and pitchforks, the handles all worn smooth from use. I felt awkward snooping around someone's home. But the fantasy that it might become mine gave me courage. Maybe the owners would leave the garden tools for me. I had noted that, except for the apple trees and four wintry azaleas between the hedge and the house, there were no other plantings.

Alongside the garage the backyard was stubbly winter grass bordered by a low wood fence. Past it, a field stretched to the next road and across that through the gray rain we could just barely see headstones in a cemetery. The yard was not deep, but I pictured a cottage garden appropriate to the antique house. Hollyhocks in a tall row along the fence might be all I needed. Who needs anything more than hollyhocks?

At one end of the fence was a weathered wooden outhouse with a shingle roof and traces of white paint. I peeked inside and discovered it was a three-seater. It was dry, no leaks, and there was a cobwebby roll of toilet paper hooked onto the side wall.

"How long has that been hanging there?" Edwin said, peering over my shoulder.

"Do you think maybe the house doesn't have a bathroom?" I wondered aloud.

A small grape arbor supporting one very old vine with a massive trunk filled the space between the outhouse and a wooden shed, which was aged to a silvery patina. Inside were scattered remnants of other peoples' lives: dusty kegs of homemade wine, a well-used dartboard with one dart still stuck in it, tame Vargas-style pinups, a faded yellow tourist banner of Orient Point. I had once considered becoming an archaeologist, following in Freddie's footsteps, but since it was the romance and not the scholarship that lured me, I did not pursue that career. Still, any type of artifact, even the broken handle of a teacup, conjured up for me whole fantasies of how people lived in the past. Even before seeing the inside of the house, I began to sense its generations of habitation.

The real estate agent arrived. He herded us out of the rain to the back of the house, where an overhang extended the flat roof. Then, with a very old-fashioned key, like one that might open a treasure chest, he unlocked a door into a small room with peeling wainscoting. He called it a mud porch. There in front of me was the wooden sink mentioned in the book of historic houses, worn shiny from use, and on it stood a faded blue woven basket filled with weather-beaten

wooden clothespins. It occurred to me that the clothespins
might be older than I was.

The next room was slightly larger, with damp wallpaper
hanging off in patches. Old bed frames, chairs, and other odd
bits of furniture were piled up to the ceiling, which was leaking. A narrow door tucked close to one wall led to the next
room, again a little larger, with one window facing north and
a tiny old-fashioned bathroom at the opposite end—the only
bathroom in the house. I was glad to see it.

The house had more rooms than I had expected, all small.
There was indeed an upstairs, with four rooms that might be
guest bedrooms someday. I pictured iron headboards, fat pil-
lows, featherbeds, antique quilts draped over the backs of
rockers. I might leave charming old books on the night tables,
next to decorated water pitchers in mismatched bowls, cross-
stitched face towels, and blocks of handmade soap.

The little eyebrow windows sat so close to the floor, beneath a sloping ceiling, that I had to kneel to look out of them,
but they did offer a view over Village Lane. The walls were
an old type of plaster full of horsehair. It crumbled easily
where I touched it. Back downstairs, in one spot where the
plaster had fallen away in a big chunk, the agent showed me
rough hand-hewn lathing, which he said dated the house to
around 1700.

The rooms were gloomy and damp. Rain was leaking in,
and plaster ceilings hung in loose swathes like inverted para-
chutes. Rotting linoleum curled up at the corners. Floorboards
sagged under my feet. But those floorboards were wide, worn
to a velvety smoothness by centuries of comings and goings,
and the irregular small windows had panes of old glass delightfully wavy and bubbled, like ones I had once seen in an Eliz-
abethan cottage in the English countryside. Through them I
saw black winter earth and bare azalea branches promising

spring, images romanticized by the imperfections in the glass.

I knew that if I didn't find some way to buy this house, someday I would be sorry.

I was thirty-eight. I would have preferred to take such a major step with a life partner. I had wonderful friends—in the true meaning of the word: loyal, caring, helpful, cheering—more good friends than anyone might ever hope for. But no one had ever said, "I want to spend the rest of my life with you." I'd begun to think that since I hadn't found love by then, I was never going to.

The house on Village Lane, in its empty field, containing within its walls so many histories of lives long past, lives and deaths, affected me deeply. It was time to get on with life, even if it was to be as a single person. At least on weekends I would have my own garden, where I could plant anything I wanted and care for it and watch it grow, in peace, far away from the daily realities and disappointments in Manhattan.

Ever since college, in the late sixties, when finally it seemed possible to live openly as a gay man, I had been searching for romance. All my friends said I was being too particular. They didn't understand. It was more complicated than that. I just did not fit comfortably into the gay lifestyle. I was looking for one special friend. But in those days, most of the gay men I knew wanted unlimited and unrestricted sex, not romantic love, and definitely not a monogamous relationship. It wasn't a moral issue for me. I felt everyone should do as he pleased. In the years before we knew about AIDS, it was not a health issue, either, although there was some contagious amoeba thing going around that did scare me. It was just that sexual freedom did not interest me. I wanted romance. The baths and the trucks, those New York meccas for anonymous sex, were as exotic to me as the tundra and the steppes: I might be interested in a travelogue, but I wouldn't want to go there myself. I went to the Continental Baths once, but that was for Eleanor Steber's concert, and I was dressed in a suit and tie, which I kept on. Steber, a legendary operatic soprano, was past her prime, but she put on a good show. She had draped a white bath towel toga-fashion over her black concert gown, and of course she sang *"Vissi d'arte,"* an aria I frequently sang to myself when no one was within hearing: *I lived for art, I lived for love . . . why, oh why, Lord, why do you repay me like this?*

I was celibate for years at a stretch. Into my early thirties, I despaired of my situation. One day, I think it must have been in 1976, on the spur of the moment—the only way I could have done it, because if I'd thought about it, I would never have gone through with it—I placed a personal ad in the *Village Voice.* This was a daring step for me. I was shy and uneasy with strangers, but I figured that as long as I was doing it, I would write the most honest and explicit ad (not sexually explicit, as some other ads were) I could come up with. It was a very long ad, headed "Monogamous Gay Man." I described myself without airbrushing: five foot eight, trim but not athletic, blue eyes, glasses, blond hair thinning prematurely. I listed things I loved: long walks in the park or on the beach, opera (but only romantic Italian opera), plants (I had no garden, but every windowsill in my sunny rent-controlled apartment on Manhattan's West Side was filled with potted plants, and I had an enormous avocado tree that I had grown from a pit), and I don't remember what else. I even pointed out that I was a Capricorn with Leo rising (January 3) for whoever might find meaning in that. Most important, I made it clear that I was interested only in a monogamous relationship.

A week after the ad ran, I got a call from the *Voice* to come down to their offices for my responses, and to bring a couple of shopping bags: there were more than three hundred letters. Stunned and intrigued that so many men had responded, I decided to meet everyone who had written more than just a name and a telephone number. For a few months, every night I had dinner—and breakfast, lunch, and tea, too, on my days off—with one man after another. I always made it clear in our preliminary telephone conversations that this would be *just* a meal, so that there would be no anxiety or expectations on either side. Three weeks into this schedule I was exhausted, and disillusioned. Even though I met some extraordinarily interesting men—one who returned lions to the wild from captivity in Africa, one who had had the first operation using pig tendons in humans to heal his shattered legs after a terrible car accident—sharing the desire for a monogamous relationship did not equal being attracted to each other. But I soldiered on.

I was encouraged that there were so many of us who felt the same way. Urged on by a few of the men I had met, I started a weekly discussion group that I labeled the M-G-M Club (Monogamous Gay Men). After a few weeks of listening to the same complaints about the stereotypical gay lifestyle, I didn't want to hear about it anymore. Frustrated, I turned the group over to one of the other men. I knew exactly what I was looking for: a best friend who was also an affectionate lover, a friend who shared my deepest yearning to be someone special for someone special. Sitting and talking about it once a week, week after week, was not going to get me anywhere. I gradually began to accept that I might be alone for the rest of my life.

•

I closed on the house on Village Lane on an exceptionally mild and sunny blue-sky March day in 1983, feeling both thrilled about the new adventure and scared about embarking on it alone. My mother had lent me the down payment, and the sellers held the mortgage, because no bank would give me one on my artist's erratic income. That day, I wasn't thinking about finances. Edwin walked over from his house carrying two boxed Jackson & Perkins roses, 'Peace' and 'Blaze', one under each arm, and Freddie and Sylvia arrived with a bottle of Moët. The real estate agent drove out from his office. We had a champagne toast outdoors from plastic glasses, which sparkled like real crystal in the sunshine.

"I'm coming back tomorrow with a crowbar!" Sylvia, always ready to renovate or redecorate, warned me enthusiastically. "Freddie and I will knock down all the loose plaster. If you don't get started on the renovations immediately, you'll put it off forever!"

My mind was not focused on fixing up the house. I was already daydreaming about the flowers I might grow. The house needed a garden. I needed a garden.

I wandered away from the champagne party to search the ground, my very own earth now. Along the fence near the outhouse I discovered tough red shoots breaking through to the March sunshine. I recognized them as peonies—we had a few of them in our backyard in Riverdale, along one side of a flagstone patio—and I guessed by the massive size of the clump that this peony had been growing undisturbed for many years. Finding those vigorous, sturdy shoots on my new property filled me with the certainty that I would have a lovely small garden, with those very peonies as the centerpiece.

At that moment the real estate agent walked over.

"You do know that this fence is not the end of your property, don't you?" he asked. "You go back about another hundred feet." He motioned over the fence toward the sunny field that stretched out almost to the cemetery.

I hadn't known that. I had happily purchased what I thought was a modest piece of property, bordered by the fence running along the backyard. Now my imaginary small garden spread out in every direction. Longer and longer fantasy borders stretched into the distance, with all sorts of nostalgic flowers popping up out of the ground, bursting into bloom the way they do in animated films, dancing and singing, and now shrubs sprang up, too, unfolding their branches, blossoming, and trees—evergreens, spring-flowering trees, fall-flowering trees, trees in full autumn color—rocketed toward the clear sky like fireworks, a leafy backdrop for my imagined chorus of dancing larkspur, delphiniums, foxgloves, and bells of Ireland, all alive with the buzzings of a garden.

A Garden Behind a Hedge

Trace your finger down a globe along the Atlantic coast where North America is jigsawed into states. Stop at the crooked crab claw New York sticks out to meet your finger in the ocean. There, at the furthest tip of the top part of the claw, is our garden.

I am keenly aware of where our garden sits on the surface of the world. Standing in its midst facing east, I imagine I can feel the earth spinning on its axis. Directly across the ocean is Rome with its balconies swathed in bougainvillea and its dusty palm trees. The daytime sky above me was bright over Rome's palms only a few hours ago, and by nighttime here it will be bright over China's cinnamon-scented rhododendrons.

Sometimes a small, noisy pleasure plane dips low over our garden. I resent its disturbing the empty air overhead and wasting fuel. But I do imagine what our garden must look like from up there: a tiny colorful clearing wedged into the puffy green treetops of the woods that have grown up in the lot behind us, textured like the miniature sponge trees dotted around my childhood model train tracks. If I fly higher out into deep velvet space, our garden is lost somewhere in the blue-and-green spinning world. But I know it's there.

•

Orient is almost surrounded by water, with the Long Island Sound to the north and several bays to the south. All that water moderates the climate. One local old-timer told me that we get more hours of sun here than anywhere else in the Northeast. He explained that it was because the South Fork holds the clouds coming in from the Atlantic and the Connecticut coast holds the clouds coming across the continent. Whether or not this is true, I have seen Connecticut across Long Island Sound blanketed under gray rain clouds, have heard on the radio that it is pouring in the Hamptons, have spoken to friends in Manhattan who tell me it is raining there, and yet all the while it is brilliantly sunny in Orient.

The North Fork's remarkably rich black loam was carried down by the last glacier, along with the massive boulders that punctuate our pebble beaches. Then, too, for generations, families buried their kitchen refuse in garbage pits on their own properties, leaving deep compost, creating some of the finest farmland in the country. Potatoes, corn, and pumpkins might be what come to mind, but the local produce includes all the trendy vegetables, bok choy to tomatillos. Organic farming is becoming popular, the local vineyards have begun to produce world-class wines, and the first truffle farm was just planted.

I discovered early that plants grow startlingly fast here. Visitors to our garden find it hard to believe that none of the trees were here when I bought the property. They are amazed that I planted the forty-foot Norway spruce in 1984 as a three-inch seedling from a "wildlife packet" that I had ordered from the nearby Cornell Cooperative Extension, incredulous that it's not a hundred years old.

Mona, my neighbor on the north side when I moved in, a

slender, pretty woman in her sixties with wide, kind eyes and big round glasses mended with Scotch tape, had her own theory as to why my garden produced such lush growth.

"They say this was an old Indian sacred burial ground," she told me.

Plants have intrigued me since as far back into my childhood as I can remember. I was three when my family moved in 1948 from an apartment building in Washington Heights, in Manhattan, to a modern redbrick house on a corner lot in Riverdale, on the southern tip of the Bronx. The only greenery around the apartment building had been two scraggly rose of Sharons struggling in shade, on either side of the entrance, right outside our windows. They reached for the sun but were stuck where they were, and I think that even as a child I empathized with their striving to get somewhere sunny and warm, far away from cement sidewalks. Looking back, our new home's front lawn and backyard were also unremarkable, but to my child's eyes they were a vast new territory. I felt a bond with the earth, with the small stones I found in it, and with the plants that grew out of it. I didn't know what to do about any of this.

The Riverdale lawn and foundation plantings survived only because we occasionally had a maintenance man—Tony, a rugged Italian American. I liked to watch him through the slats of my bedroom window blinds. As he mowed and raked, I indulged in naïve fantasies of how we might find ourselves alone together. I never once spoke to him, but I scripted many conversations that usually ended with my convincing Tony to take a shower in our basement bathroom. That was the extent of it, because going into my teens I knew absolutely nothing about sex, heterosexual or homosexual. My family never uttered a word about anything so intimate. What little I knew about romance I had learned from black-and-white movies on television, on *The Early Show* and *Million Dollar Movie*. Romance usually ended tragically and love was rarely requited. Only in screwball comedies did love win out. I wanted my life to be a screwball comedy, starring Cary Grant.

Every fall, I helped my father plant a straight row of tulip bulbs on either side of the asphalt driveway leading to our two-car garage. All winter, I anticipated the multicolored tulips that bloomed wondrously, but reliably, every spring. No thought had been put into the color scheme. We had planted the bulbs as they came out of their mesh bag. The few random black tulips among all the spring colors especially fascinated me, with their diamond-dusted sparkle and black pollen, which would smear my nose when I inhaled their sharp fragrance. In those days I used to watch *Dark Victory* whenever it was shown on television, waiting for, but dreading, the moment when Bette Davis went blind while she was planting bulbs in her garden. It was a bright, sunny day, but she thought a storm cloud had passed overhead, and yet she could still feel the sun on her hands. Bette, and we who were watching, knew this meant her brain tumor was finally going to kill her. Because my mother suffered from terrible migraine headaches and was convinced that she herself had a brain tumor (she didn't, but she had me worrying about it), this scene popped into my mind whenever I got on my hands and knees to plant tulips with my father. Any passing cloud was worrisome.

My parents were not gardeners. We mowed the lawn in summer with a push mower that got caked with damp grass, and in the fall we raked the leaves from the maples that lined our street. I liked to jump into the piles of leaves, to feel their particular crunch and smell their particular pungency. Back then, we were allowed to burn the leaves, but huge piles collected along the curb, too. Each year my mother warned me not to play in those piles, scaring me with tales of children who got crushed by the neighborhood trucks that swept up the leaves.

Once or twice a year my father drove me to Rosedale Nursery, about half an hour north of Riverdale. My father smoked a cigar in the car and I'd get carsick, but I was willing to endure that for the chance to wander among thousands of plants, every one for sale. As soon as spring unfolded, I looked forward to the Easter-egg-colored groundcovers, flat as spilled paint, carpeting the hills on either side of the nursery entrance with magenta, violet, and yellow. Were they creeping phlox and alyssum? Aubrietia?

These were the only times I enjoyed being with my father. He wanted me to play catch with him and to go to ball games. I know it hurt him that I refused. I was a stubborn child. I preferred to be by myself, daydreaming and then drawing pictures of what I had dreamed about. I resented being disturbed out of my fantasy world to be called back to the reality of our middle-class existence. But I'd go with him gladly to Rosedale.

I did have one early success as a gardener. When I was about five, I planted a peach pit in the narrow bed alongside our flagstone patio, where nothing much grew except the peonies. My parents humored me with encouragement, and to everyone's amazement, including mine, the pit sprouted, grew into a small tree, and eventually produced a peach, which I offered to my mother to eat. She said it was delicious, but I wasn't sure she was telling the truth. It was a mingy little peach, hard and misshapen. I wouldn't take a bite out of it myself.

I did have one early success as a gardener.

My mother was a tall, big-boned woman, overweight in the manner of bosomy opera singers, a look referred to in those days as "statuesque." The most vivid image I have of her in the yard is when she once caught her finger trying to unfold a lawn chair, terrifying me with her screams. I can still see the gaily striped canvas of the chair, which should have been cheery but became menacing in her hands as she flailed this way and that. Because she was so big, her exaggerated reaction was all the scarier, especially to a little child.

My mother painted floral still lifes. She was good but modest about her work. She framed only a few of her oils and watercolors, bouquets of chrysanthemums or lilacs in interesting vases, and gave them to her sisters. I have one of her watercolors hanging in Orient, a bunch of purple grapes in front of a Chianti bottle. To this day, one of the grapes is hands-down the best-painted grape I have ever seen, her use of color and wash suggesting the translucent matte surface in a few economical strokes. It calls to my mind the tale of the ancient Greek art contest between Zeuxis and Parrhasius, the most famous painters of their day. The story goes that Zeuxis's fruits were painted so realistically that birds flew down out of the sky to peck at them. I have my mother's painting in the mud porch, so I see it whenever I come in from the garden.

My father used to bring home porcelains he found in the dusty little antique shops that in those days lined Third Avenue. Most of the pieces had floral motifs, either appliquéd raised flowers or hand-painted romantic gardens filled with women frolicking or perched on garlanded swings. At either end of the living room couch we had a pair of lamps made from eighteenth-century porcelain urns, painted with garden scenes in the style of Watteau, sunlit glens surrounded by evocative shrubbery. These were the gardens I wished were outside our back door. I liked to stare at those merrymakers costumed in embroidered waistcoats and panniered gowns. I made up stories about what was going on in those gardens, putting myself there, dressed appropriately. It was time travel, and I didn't like coming back.

The day I closed on my three-hundred-year-old house on Village Lane, I was already imagining appropriately old-fashioned gardens in my empty back field, inspired by porcelain Watteaus, children's book illustrations, and movie sets. I looked up and down this street that was my new address. To my right was the Civil War monument with its American flag brilliantly sunlit against the blue March sky; across the lane and on both sides were the equally old homes of my neighbors. Were they watching from behind parted curtains?

"I'm just wondering," I asked the real estate agent while I walked him to his car. "What will it be like for a single gay man here on Village Lane?"

"It's a fishbowl," he said, and drove away.

I soon discovered that my house would continue to be known as the Soito house. In Orient, a family has to have been here for at least a generation before its name gets associated with anything. Mr. Soito lived in this house until he died. After that, it was vacant for a few years, and then I bought it from his son, Joe, who had grown up in it. It was Mr. Soito's furniture that was piled to the ceiling when I first looked at the house.

My neighbor Mona told me that Mr. Soito—Stosh, as he was known in town—was famous for his tomatoes and for his peonies. She showed me where Stosh's tomato patch used to be, in the field beyond the fence, near the outhouse, where weeds were already tall.

"You'd better start mowing soon," she warned, her big round glasses giving her the expression of a startled owl, "otherwise you'll need to get a tractor in here."

Lawn mower, I wrote on my list.

"I hope you'll grow tomatoes," she added. "Stosh always let me pick as many as I wanted."

Mona and her husband, Wendell, were reclusive, Wendell more so, but they were welcoming toward me. I thought of them as "the elderly couple next door." Now that I have been here a quarter of a century, new neighbors live in Mona and Wendell's house. They are in their thirties, as I was when I bought the Soito house. Charles and I are now "the elderly couple next door."

Mona quickly became too friendly. After a workweek in Manhattan, I started my gardening early Saturday morning, when only birdcalls interrupted the quiet. This was my time to be alone with myself—planning, digging, planting, and meditating. Mona could see my yard from her kitchen window, and as soon I left my back porch she'd come over in her bathrobe and slippers with a cigarette between her fingers. I'd be on my hands and knees on newly turned earth, when I'd see a bunny slipper step into my peripheral vision. Mona bought her clothes at yard sales, even her wigs, which she changed with her outfits rather than do up her hair, and she had many pairs of slippers and many bathrobes. I got to know them all.

Mona seemed glad to have a new audience for her Orient stories. That first April she told me how beautiful the peonies were going to be.

"Gosh, wait'll you see them! They're as big as basketballs," she said. "I'd always bring armloads of them into my house. Stosh didn't care."

Stosh's peonies, when they opened that May, turned out to be 'Festiva Maxima', the famous old-fashioned white-flecked-with-red peony that has been a favorite for generations, the most deliciously perfumed of all peonies.

That first summer, I wanted to encircle the garden with larkspur in long blue borders. As a child I once found among my sister's books a Nancy Drew mystery called *The Password to Larkspur Lane*. That title conjured up for me a dusty country road lined with tall spires of blue flowers (I didn't know exactly what larkspur looked like), crackling in the summer heat with the buzzing of bees and the mica glints of dragonflies, the blue of the larkspur rippled by wavy heat mirages, an image that epitomized a carefree summer day. I tried to re-create the effect. I couldn't afford all the plants I wanted, so I grew most of them from seed: the larkspur, of course, and also columbine, foxglove, and poppies. But I was an amateur. Seedlings died off in their flats while I was in the city. The house was too cold for them, the windows not sunny enough. I didn't yet know about heating pads and grow lights. I learned the hard way about "damping off," that scourge of seedlings. Worse, the seeds I sowed directly in the garden got lost amid vigorous weeds.

The garden began to take form in the open field, and here and there a flower developed as I imagined it would, or surprised me with voluptuousness beyond my expectations. A hollyhock bloomed in a pale orange shade—just once and never again. An unlabeled seedling sent up a fiddlehead-shaped stem dangling bright blue bells. I had no idea what it was and still don't.

That winter, on a Sunday-evening bus back to the city, the passenger in the next seat was leafing through a magazine—page after page of roses unlike any I had ever seen. I am not usually nosey toward strangers on public transportation, but I asked to borrow it. The magazine was *Yankee*; the article was about antique roses. In 1983, I had never heard of such things. It wasn't just the roses that were fabulous. The *names* of the roses intrigued me: 'Chapeau de Napoléon', 'Souvenir de la Malmaison', 'Twice-Blooming Rose of Paestum', evocative names and places I used to daydream about in high school history classes when I should have been memorizing dates of battles. On that bus trip to Manhattan, I began to envision a rose garden appropriate to the antiquity of my home, all roses grown before 1800. I copied down the nurseries that sold them, ordered catalogues, made my list. In books about these antique roses, once so beloved and now almost lost to cultivation, I learned that Empress Joséphine, Napoléon's wife, ordered her roses from British nurseries for her garden at Malmaison (in spite of or *to spite* her husband?), and that during the height of hostilities between England and France, the Royal Navy had orders to allow any ships carrying Josephine's roses to pass through their blockade. My house was already a hundred years old when Josephine was planting her roses. History, which had eluded my interest in school, suddenly started to take shape in my garden.

I planted fifty rosebushes. Each had a historic provenance; each promised a legendary fragrance. 'Cardinal de Richelieu', 'Madame Isaac Pereire', and 'Hugh Dickson' all went into the same bed, a ménage à trois. I planted 'Red Grootendorst' in the gap in the hedge, where it would grow tall together with the privet, advised by a rosarian that this rose was vigorous enough to compete with the privet's roots. The fifty young rose plants were tiny, but my research assured me they would bloom that June.

Maddeningly, that spring, Tromploy, Inc., got its first important international commission. We were hired to design murals for a new Italian restaurant in Tokyo called Chianti, typical Italian scenes: vistas glimpsed through stucco arches, Lombardy poplars disappearing in forced perspective into the distance, the placid Mediterranean stretching beyond. We had to be in Japan in May and June, just as my new baby roses were blooming for the first time. I was desolate. Our Japanese hosts tried to cheer me with lavish bouquets of rare peonies, but I felt as if my heart were being ripped out. Edwin took photographs for me, so I did get to see pictures of the little rosebushes' first blossoms. But I did not experience their famous fragrances. I promised myself I would never miss another June in Orient.

My garden became my companion, and my devotion to it entranced Mona. She didn't know much about plants. Along with her clothes and wigs, she got her houseplants at yard sales. She stuck plastic tulips of every color into her yard before any real ones came up. One fall I planted orange tulips, 'General de Wett' and 'Princess Irene'. Their spring display inspired her, so the next fall she planted orange tulips, too. To encourage her new interest in gardening, I bought her a clematis called 'Ramona', which she killed before the year was out.

One morning, from my upstairs window, I saw Mona come out her kitchen door carrying a covered plate. She marched across my newly seeded beds to my back door and let herself into my house without knocking. I heard her puttering around in the kitchen. I was flabbergasted. As soon as I saw her leave, I rushed downstairs to find that she had left on my stove a divided plastic plate, like one for a TV dinner, covered with aluminum foil. Inside were a baked potato, some macaroni, and homemade applesauce. I was touched by Mona's kindness, but I was also panic-stricken that I might never have any privacy at all from this neighbor. I remem-

bered the real estate agent calling Village Lane a fishbowl. I
didn't want to offend Mona, but I marched right over to her
porch, not sure exactly how I was going to handle it except
that I'd start by thanking her for the food.

"Oh!" she said, opening her kitchen door. "I thought you
were taking a shower so I didn't want to disturb you."

That gave me an idea.

"When I'm home alone, I often walk around the house
without any clothes on," I warned her. It wasn't true, but I
figured it would keep her out.

"Oh, that wouldn't bother me at all," she said.

Little by little I found myself looking forward to Mona's
visits, to her anecdotes about life in Orient, to her homemade
applesauce, to the funny old sweaters she would buy me at
yard sales for twenty-five cents.

"If you don't like them, you can always use them for gardening," she'd say.

My weekend routine was to be alone in my garden all day.
But something was disturbing me. At friends' parties, almost
everyone was with a partner. I had convinced myself that it
wouldn't matter that I was single, but it turned out that being
"the single person" began to wear me down. The effect was
cumulative and insidious. Eventually I began dreading dinner parties. I'd look across the table at couples who had been
together for years, who were still in love, who would go home
together to a house they shared. By the end of the evening, no
matter how pleasant my friends might be, my mood would
descend into an uneasy mix of admiration, envy, and anger,
which made me feel somehow inadequate. I would go home
wondering why I was alone when what I wanted more than
anything in the world was a special friend. Could I be so very
unattractive? What was wrong with me?

Every once in a while, I would decide to make another attempt at meeting someone. But in the early 1980s, AIDS appeared and frightened me away from dating. Friends who only a few months before had been healthy, athletic, handsome young men sickened and died. My partner at Tromploy, Inc., lost every friend who had shared his summer rental on Fire Island. He and I both tested negative, which, although a relief, made me even more cautious. I had been given a gift—a clean bill of health—and I didn't want to put that at risk.

Then the economy dipped as the decade advanced. Our decorative painting company struggled—our product was after all a frivolous luxury. Now we found ourselves having to put money into the business, to cover rent and utilities and supplies. I began to worry about my mortgage. I fretted about being able to keep the house in Orient. The idea that I might lose my new garden and have to go back to being a lonely gay man in Manhattan dismayed me.

Worse still, my mother, now in her eighties, began an inexorable descent into dementia. She had been widowed in her fifties and never remarried. Her children had been her only interest in life, which manifested itself as stifling possessiveness. I was the youngest, the last to leave home. Living across town from my mother in Manhattan, I was still the closest. Each morning before work, I would go from my West Side apartment to her apartment on East Eightieth Street to try to get her to bathe and to prepare a lunch for her. I'd stop by on my way home and find that she had not eaten. She resisted our attempts to hire someone to help her. She did not want a stranger around the house and was determined about it. Even as a younger woman, my mother veered easily into wildly melodramatic hysteria, which was terrifying to us and left us unable to console her. Now, because of entrenched family dynamics, we didn't force the issue of getting outside help.

My mother's short-term memory deteriorated rapidly. Sometimes I would come home from visiting her to find my entire message tape filled in the half hour since I had been there with terrified pleas to call her. Sobbing, she asked over and over why she hadn't heard from me in so long. Even though I called right away to assure her, she would telephone me every few minutes throughout the night, the phone ringing as soon as I set it back into its cradle. I had to answer, in case there was a real emergency, but each time she would simply say, "Hello, darling, how are you?" as if we hadn't spoken in days. I would have to be alert all night for her telephone calls. It made me desperate. I wanted to yell at her, but I couldn't, because she didn't know what she was doing. Trying to remain patient wore me out.

We did finally convince her to let us get someone to sit with her during the day, seven days a week, to do her shopping, and to bathe her and feed her. But she still called me all night long. Only during the day in my Orient garden did I find an escape. When I was on my knees, close to the rich earth, crumbling it through my fingers, pressing seeds into it, my cares seemed to have stayed back in Manhattan. I spent all day Saturday, from early morning until dark, and Sunday until it was time to return to the city, weeding, pruning, and planting. I lavished on my garden all the love, nurturing, and imagination I would have liked to shower on a partner.

One day Mona returned from a get-together with some of her Orient friends. She came directly to find me in my garden. I could tell something was troubling her.

"How was your party?" I asked, leaning on my rake.

At first she demurred, but then she said, "They were commenting on how terrible it is that so many gay couples are buying houses in Orient these days." That was the first time the topic had come up between us, and I went on guard, scared by where the conversation might lead. But Mona's big eyes were gentle behind her owl glasses. "I just said to them, 'Love is love!' And then I got up and walked out."

It was her way of letting me know it was all right with her. I was deeply touched. After that, she would mention attractive young men she had noticed working at local shops.

Mona knew I was lonely.

I began to grow around my loneliness the way a tree limb can grow through a chain-link fence, incorporating the sharp metal into its fiber without showing any outward signs of distress. I gardened my way into middle age, dog-earing nursery catalogues, circling seed packets I wanted to order, lusting after rare plants. I was so obsessed with the garden that it became harder and harder for me to leave Orient to go back to the city on Sunday night or Monday morning. There was always something that was going to bloom on Monday that I would miss, something I had been waiting months to see. My heart ached with the thought that I would be away from my garden for five days. My garden became as demanding and manipulative as a jealous lover, and as high-maintenance.

Friends encouraged me to find a companion, but the idea of dating became daunting with the passing years. After working all day at Tromploy, Inc., and then trying to cheer up my mother, I was too tired at night to think about going on a date.

My sister and I finally hired round-the-clock care for my mother, over our mother's dramatic, sobbing objections. I sold my apartment, left Tromploy, Inc., in the steady hands of my partner, and I moved full-time to Orient. This was for the garden's sake as much as for mine. It needed my full attention. My neighbor Susan helped me with the move. Susan and her husband, Tom, lived two doors down the lane from me in the Tuthill Dwarf House, built in the mid-1800s for three sisters, Cynthia, Lucretia, and Asenath Tuthill, who were each less than forty inches tall. Of course, their house was built large enough to allow their full-sized relatives to visit, even if it appeared small from the outside. Susan and Tom had bought the Dwarf House soon after I bought the Soito house.

Susan was a rapid talker with boundless energy. Each Friday she would pass by my apartment and we'd load up her Volvo station wagon with packed boxes, lamps, bags of clothes. We'd chatter and gossip, and the two-hour drive would seem just minutes long. We made trip after trip like that, until my apartment was emptied.

To help meet the expenses of my mother's caretakers, I got a job at a nursery in Southold, a fifteen-minute drive away, where I found myself doing tasks for which I had no experience. I had never before used a professional power mower or a weed whacker. I wasn't very good with them, and I never got used to them. It was a private joke of mine that to any of the nursery clients I was just a guy pushing a mower, older than the high school kids or Guatemalans, certainly less athletic, and dressed a little peculiarly in a floppy hat. They wouldn't guess that I had graduated cum laude from Columbia, studied set and costume design at the Central School of Art and Design in London, designed stage productions in New York and Tokyo, painted sets for the Metropolitan Opera, and created murals for sprawling Park Avenue apartments. Even to me, none of that seemed to be a part of my past.

At the end of the nursery workday, my arms aching from the labor and my knees flaring from arthritis, I came home and worked in my own garden until dark. Hoeing, mowing, and composting, I turned fifty without noticing how I had gotten there, paying more attention to my trees and shrubs than to myself, only to realize one day that I was at that point in my life where I had more past than future.

I joined a writing workshop held at the nearby Greenport Library. I wrote a long novel about unrequited gay love, called *All During Never*. I had in mind a hybrid cross: (*Gone With the Wind* × *Now, Voyager*) × *Auntie Mame*. I channeled all my frustrations into its characters. It was romantic and not at all graphic, and it never got published. I also wrote bad poems about longing and loneliness, and even read them aloud at local poetry events. I don't know how I had the gall. I probably was hoping someone in the audience would take pity on me and fall in love with me.

An amazing turn of events for a dear friend gave me hope that my own dreams might yet come true. One April morning in 1991, the phone rang at four o'clock. I panicked, thinking my mother was in some desperate situation. It turned out to be my friend Martile Rowland, reporting that she had just made an unexpected debut at the Metropolitan Opera. She was now at the airport on her way back home to Colorado.

I had gotten to know Martile in the seventies. She was part of my circle of New York theater friends, a big southern girl with bright red hair and a fabulous comic flair. She was playing clubs back then, singing songs from the thirties and forties, accompanying herself on the piano. We'd get her to sing "Vissi d'arte," and when she did, everyone would go crazy, yelling, "Brava!" We all thought she'd be at the Met in no time. It didn't happen. Finally, in the late seventies, she'd had enough disappointments. She married and moved to Colorado Springs.

But in 1991, while she was visiting New York, she sang for the conductor Eve Queler, who ran the Opera Orchestra of New York and was preparing Donizetti's *Roberto Devereux* for Carnegie Hall. Queler invited Martile to understudy the florid, dramatic coloratura leading role of Elisabetta. Then a miracle happened: on five hours' notice, Martile made her Carnegie Hall debut, with all her friends scrambling to get tickets at the last minute. A few months later, the Metropolitan Opera hired her to cover the role of Elvira in Bellini's *I Puritani.*

Martile's Met debut was so last-minute that I didn't know about it until she called me in Orient at four in the morning.

"They came to find me during the first intermission," she recounted. "I was having a coffee with friends at the Grand Tier bar, and they led me backstage and sewed me into one of Joan Sutherland's old costumes."

"I'm so sorry I wasn't there," I told her.

"Skip, in my heart, you were," she said, and then she rushed off to her plane.

I was so excited for Martile that I couldn't go back to sleep. I lay awake and watched the stars fade and the sky gradually turn a clear blue over my garden, the epitome of an April morning, filling me with hope. Martile's dream had come true, long after she had given up all hope for it. I might be as lucky!

Then, about seven o'clock, I noticed Susan wandering around the garden. That wasn't odd. Friends, neighbors, even strangers, often came into the garden to have a look. I pulled on some clothes and hurried outside, bursting to tell Martile's story.

"She'd never before set foot on the stage, and she had to enter singing Elvira's mad scene without ever having rehearsed with the orchestra. The conductor was in the dressing room saying she should do the best she could and he would follow her." I was surprised Susan was not interrupting me with a million questions, but I rushed on. "They just patted her on the back and wished her luck."

"I was there!" Susan blurted out. "I saw it! I was in the city, and at the last minute some friends had an extra seat for the opera. It was fantastic! Everyone was saying, 'A star was born!' "

I had not been there to see my friend's Metropolitan Opera debut, and Susan, who didn't even know Martile, had!

In 1995, Martile was scheduled to sing Donizetti's *Lucia di Lammermoor* at the San Diego Opera. I wanted desperately to go, but could not afford the trip. Susan knew this, and gave me a surprise party for my fiftieth birthday. As a gift, she had asked all my friends to chip in to send me to San Diego.

No one knew this, but I was going to check out San Diego as a place to live. I had to get away from Orient before *The Single Person* became my epitaph. Around that time, at one of Freddie's dinner parties, someone asked me what I would do if I did meet a man who was interested in me. Before I could answer, Freddie said, "He'd probably run like hell!" I was stunned to learn that I was entirely misunderstood, even by my sister. It was time to go somewhere new.

The San Diego trip was a disaster. To save money, I stayed with a friend of a friend, someone I'd never met before, an older gay man who had something negative to say about everything and was always ready with a snide remark. He was alone, and bitter about life because of it. His dissatisfaction gave him a perpetually pinched, angry expression, punctuated by eyes that were sad and desperate and resentful all at once. I found myself thinking, with dismay, *That is* me *in twenty years.*

One afternoon I wandered aimlessly through the glistening palm trees and silvery eucalyptus of San Diego's city park, obsessing about being alone. My friends might one day see *me* as a bitter old man with whom no one could bear to spend a minute. The thought made me crazy. Lucia went mad in every performance, driven insane by a thwarted love. But at least she *had* a love, thwarted or not. And she had a husband, too, even if she did stab him to death in the last act. So what was she complaining about?

A massive six-lane highway ran through the park under a pedestrian bridge. I was drawn to that bridge again and again. Finally I leaned far over the railing to watch the terrible traffic speeding beneath me. What would it be like to jump?

Only the thought of my garden saved me.

The garden to which I returned was now twelve years old. I had been presented with a blank canvas, a large one at that. For an artist, this was ideal. I gardened the way I painted: I began with a picture in my mind and then I figured out how to create it. The only difference was that my colors and textures were living beings with a thirst for life; they would grow every which way once I had placed them on the canvas.

I had no intention of ever finishing the painting. I didn't want a garden that was put in one-two-three according to a plan and then maintained pristinely forever. No foundation plantings, clipped low, treated like children who were meant to be seen and not heard. The pictures I had in my mind were of mature gardens, generations old and somewhat untended, overgrown nearly to wildness. I wanted to see this in my lifetime. However, I didn't have the money to buy mature specimen trees and shrubs. Neither did I have the time to achieve this, with only weekends in Orient. So the garden ambled along as a work in progress.

It started as three long borders outlining the rectangular open field on the north, east, and south. I grew plants from seed, accepted cuttings and divisions from friends and neighbors, and ordered what I could afford, actually more than I could afford, from familiar mega-nursery catalogues like Wayside Gardens and Parks Seeds.

One summer long before I had a garden of my own, I painted sets for the opera house in Central City, Colorado, where valleys blanketed with wildflowers nestled in every dip of the Rockies. On my days off, I wandered knee-deep through fields of sky blue columbine and vermilion Indian paintbrush, looking down from higher valleys onto lower ones, like so many Persian carpets scattered along the mountainsides, and onto the iridescent cerulean backs of bluebirds swooping over the jumble of vivid colors. I never forgot those images. Of course, once I had my Orient garden, I had to fill it with columbine. I sowed seeds for a dozen varieties, and as many of annual poppies to stand in for the Indian paintbrush that I couldn't grow. A friend who visited the garden that summer still talks about the thousands of columbine and poppies. They were spectacular, but that was only that one summer and never again. They did reseed here and there over the years, but by then I'd planted perennials and shrubs and saplings in their place, and friends who visited in following summers remember very different gardens.

I learned about lesser-known mail-order nurseries that offered plants I'd never heard of. The British Thompson & Morgan seed catalogue was a revelation after years of Park's and Burpee's, and then Edwin cut out a *New York Times* article for me about J. L. Hudson (supposedly a *nom du jardin*), whose "ethnobotanical" catalogue offered seeds for everything from a sheep-eating briar to Zapotec heirloom vegetables. My horizons expanded. I tried to grow eucalyptus that might survive Long Island winters (one did for several years, reaching twenty feet before a severe freeze killed it), and plants from New Zealand that obviously didn't stand a chance here (which didn't stop me from trying, and they all died). When I got my hands on a Heronswood catalogue, thick as a small-town telephone directory and with no photographs, just Dan Hinkley's seductive descriptions of plants he collected on treks around the world, from China to Chile, I stepped off the edge of known gardening into a free fall—tossing away food money at plants, most of which were destined to suffer and die.

But the plants that did survive flourished, and the garden very quickly attained that look of casual wildness I envisioned. Before I moved to Orient full-time, it was all I could do to keep the garden within bounds on my weekends. It amazed me just how much plants could grow in the five days I was away. Sometimes I returned to a jungle that actually scared me with its vigor.

The garden was my obsession, the only outlet for my passion—my way to express love.

Under a Papier-mâché Banana Tree

One late January day in 1996, just about a year after my devastating San Diego foray, my friend Steve came by the house, brandished a newspaper at me, and said, "Skip, there's an ad here in the Personals I think you should answer."

Steve and his partner, Mark, lived down near the end of Village Lane, with a view of the bay.

It was a Long Island newspaper. I wasn't familiar with it, and definitely wasn't aware of a local Personals that included gay ads. The tiny ad read, "East End Gay man, fifties," no other details, nothing about it appealing to me. In fact, I felt offended that just because there was another lonely fifty-year-old gay man in the area, Steve thought that was enough of a reason for me to meet him.

"I'm too old to start dating again. I cannot go through all the mechanics of getting to know someone new at this point in my life." I did not tell him that I had no intention of answering the ad.

"I think you should consider it."

Steve was a psychiatrist, so I gave his words appropriate weight, and chose my own carefully. "What I want is to come home and find someone sitting on my living room couch, all his clothes hanging in the closets, his toothbrush on the bathroom sink, as if he's been here for years, with no period of adjustment."

"You're being unreasonable."

When Steve left, I was about to throw out the paper, but I paused to read some other ads on the page. One longer ad intrigued me. It spoke of art and literature and music and horticulture. A personality sparkled through the words. The writer specified an age range of forty-five to fifty-five. I fit right in the middle: I had just turned fifty-one on the third of the month. That was encouraging, but I recalled the ad I had placed in the *Village Voice* twenty years earlier, and how nothing had come of it. *Oh well, why not?* I called the number. The recorded voice I listened to lilted with a slight southern accent. Impulsively, I left my own message in response, talking about my eighteenth-century house and the garden I loved so much.

For the rest of the afternoon, I tried to forget what I had done, because my imagination ran to too many different scenarios, some wonderful and some awful.

Charles called the next day. His voice immediately put me at ease. We spoke comfortably for more than an hour, pinballing from topic to topic—about gardening, of course, but also about art and music and books—as all the while I looked through my wavy-glass windowpanes at my January garden, at the buds swelling on bare azalea branches. A promise of spring.

Eventually Charles said, "Well, this has been a lovely conversation, but I don't understand why you bothered to answer my ad, with you all the way out there on the tip of Long Island and me here in Manhattan. How would we ever get together?"

"Well, then why did you put your ad in a Long Island newspaper?"

"I didn't! I put it in the *New York Native*."

The *Native* was a New York City gay newspaper. The only explanation we came up with was that the Long Island newspaper must have gleaned ads from it and other papers to fill up its Personals page, and just by chance the one page that Steve had brought over that day happened to include Charles's ad. This was too extraordinary to ignore. We decided to meet.

We chose February 13 because I was going to be in Manhattan that day. It was Martile's birthday, and I planned to stay overnight with a friend who also loved Martile, so that the two of us could call her at her home in Colorado Springs. Charles said the afternoon was a good time for us to meet because he worked evenings at a restaurant.

February 13 dawned sunny and blue-skied. My winter-flowering 'Dawn' viburnum was in bloom, its blossoms bright pink in the morning light, perfuming the air, giving me hope. I'd had so many dating disappointments in my life, but since I was already planning the trip to the city, and because it was a radiant winter day, and as long as I had my garden to come home to, I didn't feel pressured by the idea of a blind date. But I decided to wear my lucky turquoise blue cap, just in case. Everyone always commented that it brought out the blue in my eyes.

On the bus into the city, I worried about whether I might have left the stove on, or left a candle flickering, or if an unexpected storm might send a tree crashing through the roof, and if my insurance would cover such events. Or if the insurance company would prove it had been my fault. I might lose the house. My mother brought me up to worry about the direst possible outcomes. She always feared that the worst would befall her children.

My mother was on my mind because I was getting out at the Sunrise Coach stop at Seventy-ninth Street and Third Avenue. This was the stop I had used when I went to visit my mother during her long illness, my stomach in knots. Just a couple of months earlier, Freddie and I had moved her to a nursing home near us on Long Island, in Riverhead. My mother had never wanted to leave her apartment, certainly not to go into a home, but now she required full-time medical attention. As soon as we made the decision and got her set up at the facility, I wished we had done it years earlier. She was well taken care of there, and we knew someone was nearby whenever she might need help. The day we finally emptied my mother's apartment and locked the door for the last time, I told myself I would never again have to come back to this neighborhood with all its desperate connotations.

Charles's apartment turned out to be exactly one block south of where my mother's Eightieth Street apartment had been, on Seventy-ninth between Second and Third. But now, as I stepped off the bus, all those years of devastating visits vanished into the brilliant Manhattan February sunshine. Mica raged like diamonds in the sidewalks, traffic flashed crisp glares off chrome and glass, apartment windows above me mirrored the cloudless blue sky. I was a tourist in a new country.

The doorman buzzed me up. I had no way of picturing Charles, except that he had told me he was tall. He was waiting at his door. In fact, he was so tall that I had to look up to meet his sparkling dark eyes. He spoke before I had a chance to feel awkward.

"There's a new Vietnamese restaurant around the corner," he said, with a touch of southern magnolias in his speech. "Miss Saigon. We'll go there for lunch. Then we'll come back here for tea." His smile was sunny and animated, dancing around his lips, immediately putting me at ease.

At Miss Saigon, a couple of blocks up Third Avenue, we sat at a table for two under a papier-mâché banana tree and told each other everything about ourselves we thought might sound alluring. Charles had gardened in Ithaca, New York, where he'd lived for six years while he worked as a maître d' at L'Auberge du Cochon Rouge, the best restaurant in the area, he explained. Now he worked at the restaurant at the Carlyle Hotel, within walking distance of his apartment. He had spent time on Barbados with his friend Richard Iverson, the director of the botanical garden on the island.

"Iverson teaches now at Farmingdale," Charles added.

I didn't say that I wasn't sure where or what that was. I found it interesting that he used last names for friends.

"I brought back a cutting of a rare coleus from Barbados," Charles went on, "wrapped in my wet bathing suit. We found it on the grounds of Codrington College," he explained, "the oldest university in the Western Hemisphere. I'll show you the cuttings when we go back up to the apartment."

I was glad to hear that our date was still going to continue past lunch.

"Now I garden the two tree pits in front of my apartment building, but there's nothing to see in them in the middle of winter," he apologized.

"In Orient, my 'Dawn' viburnum is blooming right now."

I described the shrub and went on and on about the garden in Orient. How thirteen years earlier I had wanted it to be appropriate to the eighteenth-century house, a cottage garden brimming with delphiniums and cleomes. How over the years I added more and more antique roses until there were over three hundred. How the garden had now evolved into over-the-top lushness as I ordered practically every unusual new plant I found in catalogues.

While we ate banana ice cream under the faux banana trees, I wondered if I was talking too much about my garden, if Charles was getting bored, and if I was still invited up for tea. But then, when the waiter brought us tea, Charles asked for the check instead and told him we'd be having our tea at home. We split the bill, and I was pleased to see he was a generous tipper.

When Charles tells the story of our first meeting, he says he was wracking his brain trying to come up with as many garden references as he could to keep me interested. I wasn't aware of that at the time. He seemed entirely at ease.

Back upstairs in Charles's apartment, I commented on the chartreuse walls of his living room. They glowed in the afternoon winter sun with the warmth of an August garden.

"I chose the color," Charles said, helping me out of my jacket, then gracefully taking off his coat, "but I cried when I saw it on the walls after the painters finished. When it was wet, it was a shocking psychedelic Day-Glo green. Now that it's faded a bit, I've become very fond of it."

"I like it."

With the sun streaming in, I felt like I was in a greenhouse. I noticed the coleus cuttings rooting in fine cut-glass tumblers on the windowsill. The leaves were unusual, tiny and fernlike, bronze and purple.

"When I saw the plant on Barbados, I had no idea what it was. It was huge, four or five feet tall, like a shrub," Charles explained. "Iverson identified it as a coleus. He says he never saw one like it. He wants to have it propagated, and he is adamant that it be called coleus 'Codrington College'. I plant them out in the tree-pit gardens every summer. Then, at the end of the season, I take cuttings for next year."

I commented on an odd ivory-colored cactus next to the coleus.

"That's not a cactus, it's an albino Euphorbia. It looks like white chocolate, doesn't it? That's from Barbados, too. The parent plant down there was huge. I broke off a tiny piece and smuggled it home. It grows slowly because it doesn't have any chlorophyll. I can't pronounce its proper name. I'm slightly dyslexic."

He was so eloquently loquacious, I hadn't noticed. But when I complimented him a few minutes later on his brightly patterned shirt, he said matter-of-factly, "I got it at Feline's Basement," instead of Filene's Basement, which conjured up for me such a delightfully bizarre department store that I didn't correct him.

Charles started water to boil for tea, reached easily to the highest shelves of his kitchen cabinets, for which I would have needed a stepladder, and brought down gleaming antique cups and saucers patterned with exotic gardens.

"It's the purple Palestine pattern," he explained. "English Staffordshire transferware, made in the mid-1800s." He showed me the rest of his collection of cups and saucers and plates and platters with fanciful renditions of palm trees and camels. "This is one of the rarest." He held out a platter featuring three odd giraffes. "It commemorates the first giraffes brought back to England."

Next, he showed me his Murano glass ashtrays, speckled with gold leaf, or patterned with swirls of colored glass, or embedded with bubbles like a perpetual effervescence. My family had ashtrays like those when I was a child, but over the years we had come to think of them as kitsch. They'd all been given away, or thrown out. Now, through Charles's enthusiasm, I saw them as valuable collectibles, and beautiful. I mourned ours. If I still had one, I would have been able to give it to him as a gift.

Charles swept his long arm toward the chartreuse walls

"I'm a collector," he explained.

in a gesture that indicated the many unusual prints displayed around the room, each beautifully framed, set like jewels against the vibrant color. "I'm a collector," he explained, and the word, coming from him, suddenly meant something to me that it hadn't before. I myself had always bought things that I liked, not with any idea of the individual pieces ever adding up to a meaningful whole. "I collect abstract expressionist prints of the forties and fifties," he went on. "This is only a part of the collection. The apartment is too small to show them all. There's not enough wall space."

He walked over to what I thought were elegant folding screens, tall pale wood panels patterned with darker grain in fantastic arabesques, outlined with a thin lacquer-red border. They turned out to be closet doors. When he opened one, he showed me shelving lined with carpet where he stored framed prints upright in slots. "A friend helped me design this storage system," he said. "We were originally going to paint the panels chartreuse to match the walls, but when I saw this beautiful graining we decided to just seal them with tung oil."

He slid a small, richly colored print out of one of the carpeted compartments.

"This is a Louise Nevelson. It's called *The Magic Garden*. It's a combination of etching, engraving, and aquatint techniques. And see," he continued with a flourish of his fingers, "she hand-colored it, too. It's an artist's proof, signed in pencil."

Before he put away *The Magic Garden*, I thought I saw flowers and a snake in the composition, the way my mother used to find faces in decorative patterns or animals in clouds.

He pulled out a larger vivid red and indigo print.

"This is a Dennis Beall, *In the Asparagus Patch*. Don't try to figure out why it's called that," he instructed. "These works are spontaneous and gestural, not representational."

I was glad I hadn't pretended to see something in the Nevelson.

"This is one of four, which means it was the first print of an edition of four. He made it in 1956."

"I was eleven in 1956, and I was trying to paint and draw like this, although I doubt I knew it was called abstract expressionist. We always had art books around the house, and I copied the styles."

"I'd like to see your work sometime," Charles said. "Do you still have any of the paintings?"

"I think there are some in the garage."

"The garage?" he asked, startled. "That doesn't sound very archival."

There was a stern warning implicit in his tone. Clearly Charles revered art and artists, and I guessed he did not tolerate anything less than professionalism. I imagined Charles's reaction to the casual chaos of my Orient house, if he ever came there, such a contrast to his orderly apartment. I devoted my time to gardening, not housecleaning. I quickly put the idea of his visiting out of my mind.

We moved to the table by Charles's south-facing living-room windows overlooking his dormant street gardens. Charles showed me scrapbooks with photographs of those gardens in spring, blazing with tulips, and in summer, lush with tropical elephant ears, caladiums, and cannas. One photograph, which he had taken from the window where we sat, showed the springtime tree pits as kaleidoscopically colorful geometric shapes against the gray of the pavement, long shadows of the honey locusts radiating out at odd angles. The photograph itself was stunning, as gestural in its composition as his abstract prints.

Over Earl Grey tea Charles deftly switched the conversation to long-ago relationships that hadn't worked, and why they hadn't. Neither of us felt we had ever found what we were hoping for.

"My grandmother Essie always told us kids to be particular," Charles said. "She had a house in Augusta, Georgia. One summer, she ripped out her entire lawn and planted it in solid petunias, the whole front yard. That just wasn't something you did in Augusta! We used to visit her once a year, and when we all got into our car to drive home, the last thing she always shouted to us while she was waving goodbye was 'Be particular!'"

I thought about my friends always chiding me for being too particular.

Charles talked about the hurts or disappointments in earlier relationships. I made mental notes so that I would not make the same mistakes his past lovers had made, should that situation ever arise. Not that I had my hopes up. Mostly I was thinking, *What a remarkable person. I've never met anyone like him.*

Next Charles steered us toward our family histories. Charles's mother still lived in the same house in Augusta, Georgia, to which she had moved after divorcing his father thirty years ago. She had never remarried. Charles's father had remarried, but died young of a heart attack. I told him about my mother in the nursing home in Riverhead.

"She never remarried, either, after my father died of a heart attack," I explained. "That was almost forty years ago."

"I have a sister, Frieda, who is an artist," Charles continued.

"My sister's name is Freddie, and she is an art historian. She's an artist, too! She paints Orient landscapes."

"I have a brother, Bill," he said. "He's an engineer."

"I have a brother, Bill, too! He's an architect. He's the only one in the family who has children."

Charles said, "Bill is my only sibling who has children, too. I have another sister, Angel. She's a singer. She had a career for a while in New York. She used to sing with a group called the Last Roundup. Now she's married and living in Providence. She's not singing much anymore. It's a shame because she's riveting onstage."

"She shouldn't give up," I said. "I have a friend, Martile, who is an opera singer. She got married and gave up on her career, too, but now she's singing around the world!" I told Charles about Martile's amazing career. "I'm thinking about going to Atlanta in May to hear her in *Trovatore*."

"Let's go see it together!" he exclaimed. "My brother lives in Atlanta. We can stay with him."

I'd known Charles for maybe all of three hours, but this did not strike me as improbable. To my own surprise, it seemed the logical thing to do. "Let's," I said, sipping tea from my purple Palestine cup.

"My brother is a Mormon," Charles added. "He converted. He and his wife have five Mormon children, but I'm sure it will be okay."

Before I could respond, Charles said, "You have such pretty blue eyes! Are they really yours?" He read my startled expression. "I mean, some people wear colored contact lenses."

I assured him my eyes were my own. I didn't tell him that I had positioned myself at the window so that the sky would be reflected in my eyes and make them bluer.

That night I called Martile to wish her a happy birthday. She seemed especially excited.

"Guess what!" she bubbled before I could tell her about Charles. "I'm having an iris named after me!"

"Martile, that's so fantastic! What does it look like?"

Martile didn't know much about the plant. She wasn't a gardener. But she knew I'd be thrilled.

"The breeder brought a photograph of the flower backstage after one of my performances. It's big and yellow. He said it has a red beard, whatever that means."

"It's that little fuzzy tuft on the bottom petal. I guess he was inspired by your beautiful bright red hair."

Martile promised to send me information about ordering Iris 'Martile Rowland' for my garden.

"I'm glad you're going to grow it," she said. "I'd probably kill it."

"I have news for you, too." Finally, I got to tell her about Charles. "He's from Georgia," I tossed in.

"I approve," Martile said, as I knew she would, being from Shreveport, Louisiana, herself. "And you met him on my birthday! How marvelous! We'll be able to celebrate my birthday and your anniversary on the same day!"

"The day before Valentine's Day," I added.

But I started to look at the situation more realistically. I had just met the man, had spent only a few hours with him; he was strikingly attractive, a maître d' in one of the best restaurants in New York, who must meet thousands of people. Why would he be interested in me all the way out on eastern Long Island? I convinced myself that chances were I'd never hear from him.

On the other hand, there was Martile's success to inspire me.

The next day, when I was back home on Village Lane, Charles did call.

"I'm coming out to Orient this weekend," he said in his enthusiastic, resonant voice.

After that phone call, I looked around me and panicked. Every inch of windowsill and floor space close to windows was crammed with plants in plastic pots, my tropical plants that wouldn't have survived the winter outside. Their containers sat in plastic saucers, aluminum foil food trays, chipped porcelain plates. Top-heavy shrubs and tall vines were lashed with twine to window sashes. Shriveled leaves lay in piles between the pots. Some plants were dead-looking twigs, aphids were on others. Jugs of water, turquoise with Miracle-Gro, were lined up alongside the pots. I was used to wending my way through palms and elephant ears and seed flats under fluorescent lights to get at closets or drawers, or to the refrigerator, but now, trying to imagine my home through Charles's eyes, I saw the collection of potted plants as an embarrassing obsession. He'd think I was crazy.

Roses in the Snow

There was no way I could get the house emptied of plants before Charles's visit. I could no more cram them all into one room than put them outside in the cold. The best I could do was to tidy up, not a small chore.

There were the echiums, for one thing. I'd seen pictures of them in a magazine article, gigantic spires of bright blue flowers like prehistoric delphiniums. The fact that they were also called Tower of Jewels and Pride of Madeira had made them even more intriguing to me. I'd been trying to grow them from seed, because the article led me to believe they might be hardy on Long Island. They weren't. I lost the first batch. This time I had grown them in pots and brought them inside for the winter, hoping they might bloom the following year. They were big plants with spindly branches ending in tufts of long, rank, felty leaves shaped like banana peels, each plant about the size and shape of a standard poodle in full show coat. I had about twenty pots of them at different windows throughout the house. The leaves were curling up, making crackling sounds as they fell to the floor. The dead leaves smelled like rancid peanut butter.

There was not much to be done about all this except to sweep up the leaves, vacuum, and spray the aphids. I hoped the outside garden would carry the day. I wanted Charles's first impression of the garden to be a good one, even in February.

I went outside to see what might need doing there. The winter had been mild, but that day, at least, had the look of coldness about it: gray branches against flannel skies, every hue faded by dampness so that the dark of swarming star-lings was the same dark as the red cedars. I wandered through the garden, pretending I was taking Charles on a tour. Damp-ness coated my skin, as well as the grass, branches, pine nee-dles, and stone paths, with a muted sheen.

I'd planted the garden so that there was something in bloom during all twelve months. I hoped this would impress Charles. I tried to picture him leaning across the path to press his nose into the 'Dawn' viburnum's pink pom-poms. Was he really as tall as I remembered? The witch hazels were in flower, too, cinnamon red 'Diana' and sulphur yellow 'Ar-nold's Promise' emitting their own sharp astringent per-fumes. Their flowers looked like tiny ribbons tied in bows along the branches. Would Charles know that the common drugstore witch hazel was made from this plant? I guessed he would. By the path to the back door the winter honeysuckle was covered with a haze of pale yellow buds releasing a lemony fragrance, always reminding me of the Jean Naté eau de co-logne popular in the 1960s. My sister used it back then. Would Charles ever have heard of Jean Naté? He was only four years younger than me, not so much of a difference that we wouldn't share reminiscences.

From across the garden came the unexpected mid-summery smell of the sweetbox, *Sarcococca humilis*, which can throw its scent the way a ventriloquist throws his voice, tricking you to look somewhere nearby for the source. At the far end of the garden the tiniest daffodils were already up and blooming, miniatures with perfect yellow trumpets as jaunty as 'King Alfred' but no bigger than my pinkie finger-nail, their grassy foliage only as tall as a lawn that needs mowing. A snowfall of two inches would bury them, but with a melt they'd bounce back up. So often, the smallest are the bravest. Charles must see these. I considered making a bou-quet of them, then decided they were more impressive left where they were.

As it turned out, it snowed heavily the day of Charles's visit, erasing the garden. I rushed out with a broom to free the evergreens of burdens too great for branches to bear. Paths were invisible. I worried I'd step on some small shrub. No miniature daffodils in sight.

I thought of Gladys, for a very short time our live-in maid in Riverdale. Gladys, who had come from the Caribbean, had never seen snow. When we had our first snowfall, Gladys rushed from window to window, looking out at a whiteness without boundaries where before there had been grass and paths and shrubs and sidewalks and roads defining our exis-tence. I could tell that something equally boundless was welling up inside her. She pulled on her hand-me-down woolen coat and gloves and herded us all outside, my brother and sister and me, and started a snowball fight! She won by pick-ing up a huge chunk of snow and crashing it over our heads.

Her excitement about something as common as snow made us laugh back then. Now that I have traveled to some of the Caribbean islands, I picture Gladys in the surroundings in which she had grown up, in unrelenting sun, a background of turquoise sea and shell-strewn sand, and I understand why she went wild when it snowed. In the tropics, growth and decay are simultaneous. The earth is littered with brown-ing leaves, broken branches, fading blossoms, and rotting fruits, and through it all the same plants that have dropped all these dying parts of themselves go on sending out fresh

It snowed heavily the day of Charles's visit.

shoots. There is no wiping clean the slate—no ending and therefore no beginning.

The Orient garden had been wiped clean. I thought the snow would delay the bus on the Long Island Expressway, so I didn't hurry. It's only an eight-minute drive from Orient to the bus stop in Greenport, and I planned on being there early, waiting for Charles, having the car warm and ready.

Driving, the stone gray Long Island Sound the deepest color in a grisaille landscape, I remembered the cold, snowy winters of my childhood, the crunch of snow in the creases of wet mittens, the smell of wet wool. An 8mm home movie preserves a record-breaking snowfall sometime in the late 1940s. I hadn't watched this film for thirty years, but I recalled vivid Technicolor red scarves, fedoras, ladies' hairdos imitating Irene Dunne's, my mother's fur-lined boots stepping soundlessly into snowdrifts, her dark lipstick, a quick smile close to the camera, a three-year-old me bundled up in ear flaps and mittens, family figures moving slower or faster than in life depending on the vagaries of the projector, mouse-colored bare trees in the background, dog hairs and dust on the film jumping like one-celled creatures against snow that really sparkled on the screen. I heard the clicking of film on sprockets and smelled the hot projector bulb.

Sometimes the film would get stuck and there'd be only a second to free it before that frame burned, the way the coils of my memory now sometimes snag on a long-past disappointment, and then it is wiser to speed forward before the flames start.

When I pulled into the parking lot in Greenport, I realized that despite the snowstorm the bus had arrived on time and was already gone. Charles was standing alone at the far end, at the water's edge, an isolated windblown figure dark against the snow and the leaden bay, carrying a huge bunch of red roses. My stomach still sinks when I picture him all alone there in that snowfall with those extravagant roses for me, and me not there to welcome him.

"I wanted to be here waiting for you," I told him nervously.

"A woman on the bus offered to drive me to Orient, but I didn't know where you lived," he said, folding himself into my car. "I assured her my friend was definitely coming to get me. Then when you were late and the snow got worse, I wasn't so sure anymore."

I was distressed that I'd already caused him a moment's doubt. But Charles didn't seem angry or even concerned. He was entirely at ease sitting next to me in my car. He adjusted the seat to give himself more legroom. The bouquet of roses filled all the space between Charles and the dashboard. I saw now that they were not simple red roses. The outsides of the petals were silvery and the insides a glowing garnet, like flowers in a hand-tinted daguerreotype. Charles told me their name—nothing I recognized from my rose catalogues.

We turned onto Greenport's Front Street, the main shopping area, which runs along the bay. I wondered if Charles was expecting the Hamptons.

"That's our vintage 1940s movie theater, and that's our corner luncheonette, the Coronet. It hasn't changed much since the fifties."

"It looks like fun. Let's go there for breakfast tomorrow."

I turned toward the Main Road, then east toward Orient.

"This is the causeway," I explained as the road stretched ahead of us, bordered by whitecap-laced Orient Harbor on the south and the roiling Long Island Sound on the north. Connecticut was a low purple ribbon across the choppy, cold gray water on our left. The wetlands on our right were long swathes of snow prickled with ochre beach grasses.

"That's Orient over there." I pointed past the snowy

patches of wetlands and dark bits of bay to the strip of white houses along the water's edge. "Every time I drive across here, even after all these years, I'm still overwhelmed by the beauty. No matter how preoccupied I am, I can actually feel all my cares lifting off my shoulders. It's different every time of day, and every season. In summer, it's all beach roses, and the fragrance blasts into the car as you drive past."

I wished I could conjure up for him the causeway in June: the Sound turquoise, mirror-flat under a warm sky, rugosa roses blazing on the sand dunes.

"And that's our farm stand, Latham's." It was closed for the winter, a yellow wooden skeleton, bleached like driftwood, surrounded by barren fields. Long furrows still showed through the snow, parallel lines as in a perspective drawing, leading to the icy bay in the distance, where water blurred into sky.

"In summer, it's rows of raspberries and then cabbages, and the water is bright blue behind them. They have the best corn. And tomatoes. And delicious strawberries. And the cauliflower is better than anywhere else. It tastes like chestnuts."

"I love cauliflower," Charles said.

"And here's Village Lane. That big tree is the Buttonwood Tree. They say it was here when the Declaration of Independence was signed. This is the Monument, for the local soldiers who died in the Civil War. It's called the 'War of the Rebellion' in the inscription."

"Back home it was the 'War Between the States,'" Charles said with his trace of Georgia accent. "Down there, they still don't know it's over."

"That's my house, on the left."

"It's adorable."

"Are you up for a quick tour of Orient? Or do you want to go right to the house?"

"Let's have the tour!"

I continued down Village Lane, bordered all along with eighteenth- and nineteenth-century shingle-and-clapboard homes. The drive felt like a comfortable old routine.

"That's the Country Store, where you can get sandwiches and basic supplies; otherwise you have to drive the eight minutes to Greenport, to the IGA. And that's our tiny post office, right next door."

"It's cute!"

"That's Poquatuck Hall, our meeting place for concerts and events, and these buildings are the Oysterponds Historical Society." I slowed down to point out several elegant wooden buildings that are now museums, and added, "Orient used to be called Oysterponds." I stopped in front of a greensward that sloped up to a small building. "That's the old schoolhouse. It has one room, and now they have art exhibitions there in the summer." I drove on to where we could see the bay from Village Lane. "Orient used to be a big whaling port, too. A lot of these houses were built by wealthy ship captains."

"Some of them have widow's peaks, I see."

"Widow's *walks*," I corrected him, instantly worried for having done so. To get off the subject, as I turned onto King Street, I mentioned that the King family is still around. "The story goes that at Christmas caroling time, they sing 'We Three Kings of Orient Are.' "

"Really? Are you kidding?"

"I don't know. It's just what I've heard."

I continued out into farmland, then circled around to Orchard Street, where I pointed out Freddie's house as we passed. "You'll meet her and Sylvia tomorrow. Now we're back on Village Lane, and here's the house."

I pulled into the driveway, alongside the 'Dawn' viburnum, its pink pom-poms iced over.

"The snow has covered up everything in the garden," I apologized as we got out of the car. Charles would be seeing the rooms crowded with potted plants before he saw the garden. This wasn't working out the way I had imagined. "If you'd been here yesterday, there would have been lots to show you. That pink bush blooms in the winter, and if it weren't freezing right now it would be very fragrant."

Charles leaned across and dutifully took a sharp intake of frigid air.

"And over there, there were tiny daffodils yesterday."

"It's pretty in the snow. And I'll get to see it all eventually. Let's go inside and warm up."

I thought again about Charles waiting at the bus stop in the cold, and he a Southerner. If only he had mentioned my name to that woman on the bus. She was a friend who lived down the street. Orient is such a small town that, when I ran into her a few days later in the vegetable aisle at the Greenport IGA, she already knew that I was the one Charles was coming to see. She told me how intrigued she had been by the tall handsome stranger with the roses, on his way to he knew not where. "I was going to flirt with him myself. I hope you didn't keep him waiting too long in that snowstorm!"

I led Charles inside through the back mud porch. We had to bend out of the way of the bay tree and duck under the brugmansia. "I still haven't organized all the plants," I said lamely, as if there might be some other way to cram them all into the house. "I might not bring so many inside next year."

"Why not? You wouldn't want to lose any of them."

If Charles thought there was anything odd about dragging a couple hundred plants inside for the winter, he didn't let me know. He didn't say anything about the nasty smell of the echiums, either.

We squeezed through the palms and elephant ears to the

living room. Charles made himself comfortable on my couch, and looked as if he had been at home there for years.

"Where'd you find this fabulous couch?"

It was a wonderful, big old thing, upholstered with an odd Aubusson-type tapestry depicting rolling hills and copses of trees in a sort of Arts and Crafts style, in shades of olive and ochre and faded red. I'd gotten it twenty years earlier at auction, cheap because it wasn't in perfect condition and no one else wanted it. It was in even worse condition now. That hadn't mattered to me until I saw Charles sitting on it, the tapestry splitting, a few feathers working their way out.

"I got it at Manhattan Storage Galleries, right around the corner from my mother's apartment."

"I know it well," Charles said. Of course, it was just up the block from his own apartment.

I'd furnished the house from yard sales and auctions, choosing old pieces that showed wear, because the house itself had a patina from three hundred years of usage. It just happened that the battered tables and chairs and geegaws that appealed to me were not in demand, so I was able to afford them. An end table with flaking, generations-old layers of paint, showing red under green under yellow, seemed to fit right in, no matter if one leg had been reglued and was coming loose again. Now, with Charles sitting on my dilapidated couch, it looked to me like I was living in a junk shop.

"When I come out next weekend," Charles said, "I'm going to bring you something that would look perfect hanging over this couch."

I didn't know how to answer this. The first thing that came to mind was that he was already planning to come out to see me again, which put me at ease because it meant I hadn't yet said or done anything to discourage him, and the house full of plants hadn't turned him off. But what if I didn't want whatever it was he was going to give me to hang over my couch? How would I handle that? And maybe I shouldn't accept it even if I liked it.

That evening, cozy on the couch, we watched a video of Martile's 1991 Mexico City *Roberto Devereux* at the Palacio de Bellas Artes, taped from Mexican television. I wanted so much for Charles to *get* Martile, to appreciate her talent, her voice, her dramatic intensity, as much as I did. At the end of Elisabetta's last-act aria, "Vivi, ingrato," Martile interpolated a perfect high D-flat and held it. The camera stayed close-up on her face as the audience went berserk with tumultuous applause and bravas for so long that tears began to stream down Martile's cheeks. I looked at Charles, to see if he was enjoying the performance. He was crying, too.

My own eyes welled up. I knew then for certain that the two of us would go together to Atlanta for Martile's *Il Trovatore*.

I wasn't sure what to do next, so I surprised myself by suggesting a warm bath, together. Charles surprised me by accepting the idea without hesitation.

It had been many years since anyone had seen me naked. At fifty-one I wanted to get over that hurdle as quickly as possible. I could tell from Charles's perfect posture that he was fit and trim, which made me even more insecure.

At least I had scrubbed and polished the bathroom the day before. The dingy little room I'd peeked into the first day I saw the house had been remodeled, now all white tile and unfinished pine and chrome fixtures, modern enough to look inviting, but rustic enough to fit the rest of the house. In the other rooms, I had tried to keep the old patinas the house had acquired over its three hundred years, but I wanted the bathroom to be invitingly fresh, like a Scandinavian sauna.

I drew the bath and lit a candle on the white tile ledge.

Charles settled into the steamy water, his long legs folded to fit into the small tub. I tucked myself in opposite him, while he made room for my legs as if we had been doing this together for years.

He looked into my eyes and sang, sort of, "You'd be so easy to love . . ."

I realized he couldn't sing at all, which I found adorable.

The next weekend Charles came out to Orient again. I was at the bus stop a half hour early, in case the bus was ahead of schedule. It was a good thing, because he got off the bus carrying a large, cumbersome package.

"This is what I promised you for over the couch."

At the house, he unwrapped a stunning early-nineteenth-century hand-hooked rug, its colors all the colors of my tapestry couch in a dazzling pattern suggesting acanthus leaves. Holding it in his long arms, he positioned it with the eye of a curator. I got out some faded red silk rope I'd saved from a theater production I had designed years before, and together we hung the rug above the couch. Instantly, I could not imagine the wall without it.

"We'll keep it here on loan," I said.

"No, I'm giving it to you," Charles insisted. "It's perfect for this house. This is where it's meant to be."

After that, Charles came to Orient every weekend. Our routine was instantly as familiar and comfortable as a well-worn path, as if we'd been together forever.

Mr. Soito's Peonies

One day soon after Charles's first visit to Orient, he said, "I want to meet your mother."

My mother was ninety-three, bedridden, and immobile, in the nursing home in Riverhead, a forty-minute drive from Orient. I had been going there regularly to sit by her bed, to hold her hand, to talk to her even though I could not tell if she understood or even heard me. I'd repeat over and over that she had been a good mother, that her children were all healthy and happy and she didn't have to worry about us anymore. I sang favorite songs to her, songs she had sung to me when I was little: "Mairzy Doats," "A Bushel and a Peck," and songs Kate Smith, my mother's favorite performer, made famous, like "When the Moon Comes Over the Mountain." My mother only occasionally offered a flicker of response. I wasn't sure a visit from Charles was a good idea.

"She probably won't even be communicative," I warned him. "She might not open her eyes. She might not even know who I am."

"It is only proper we should meet," he said, putting his "southern etiquette" slant on it. He knew these visits with my mother were troubling, and I understood he wanted to prove we were in this together.

Charles offered to drive to the nursing home. I hadn't ever driven a car until I bought my house, when I was thirty-eight, and was still not relaxed at the wheel. The trips to visit my mother in Riverhead were the longest I regularly made. Charles had started driving as a teenager in Tennessee. It was second nature to him, he was good at it, and he liked it. I was happy to be a passenger.

As I gave directions to the nursing home, I remembered how, before her senility, my mother had become resentful that I spent my weekends in Orient and not with her. One Mother's Day, I picked out a bouquet of red roses to have sent to her. When I telephoned from Orient on the holiday, she was crying.

"All those roses arrived with their buds snapped off," she sobbed. "You wasted your hard-earned money. You should call that florist and complain!"

I did call him. I knew he would remember me, because he had been very patient while I selected roses still in tight bud so that they would have a long vase life.

"Sir," he said, "I packed that box personally. If those buds were broken off, then your mother did that herself."

In my heart I knew he was right. She had probably been so furious I wasn't there in person to wish her a happy Mother's Day that she destroyed my bouquet.

Remembering how upset she had been, I sighed. "Her nurses told me they don't know what she's hanging on for, what's keeping her alive."

"She's got her reasons," Charles said with certainty.

"I think she worried so much about her children all her life, she probably just wants to see each of us safely dead and buried so she can be sure nothing bad can happen to us. Maybe then she'll rest in peace."

Charles laughed, thinking I was joking.

In Riverhead I directed him to turn north at the Taco Bell. My mother's nursing home was up a little hill behind it. Drifts of dirty snow polka-dotted the parking lot and framed the glass-paneled entrance. We walked along the institutional hallway, past sad people in wheelchairs staring at nothing, to the very end, to my mother's room. The door was ajar. Charles touched my arm reassuringly. We went in.

As always, everything about the room seemed dismal to me. It made me think of a cheap motel room. My mother's bed was next to a window, but it overlooked the parking lot and the piles of cement-colored snow. My mother was on her back in bed, clutching a crocheted baby blue coverlet close to her nose. It wasn't something I'd given her. I had learned from one of the nurses that schoolchildren were encouraged to donate presents to the residents, and some people knitted and crocheted gifts. I felt bad that strangers were donating things to my mother. She was always leery of strangers.

Now I was awkward, not sure how to behave in front of Charles. I said, "Momma?"

She opened her eyes and saw Charles. Her face brightened.

"What a handsome man!" she said in a strong voice I hadn't heard in years. "Come here and give me a kiss!"

Charles bent over the bed and kissed her cheek. She beamed, smiling toothlessly.

"Mrs. Wachsberger, it's so good to finally meet you," Charles said, pulling one of the hard plastic chairs close to sit by her. "Skipper has told me so much about you."

"Well, I hope it was all good things." She was almost flirtatious. I was stunned. I hadn't had a real conversation with my mother in over a year.

"Skipper tells me you used to go to the opera together," Charles went on. "Do you remember that?"

"Of course I remember," my mother said.

I sat on the other plastic chair, close to the foot of my mother's bed. I watched the two of them and felt I was in an Almodóvar film.

Charles spoke loudly to her. I realized suddenly that my mother was hard of hearing, and Charles had figured it out right away. I had never thought of this simple explanation for her unresponsiveness. I marveled as Charles drew her out with the family stories I had only recently told him, which he seemed already to know by heart. It didn't matter whether my mother remembered the past, she was involved in the moment. She was riveted to Charles as if he were a celebrity who had come especially to see her. I had once seen her radiate a similar enthusiastic joy when we by chance came upon a young John F. Kennedy greeting a crowd of supporters, even though my mother would have only voted Republican, if she voted at all. Attractive men brought out a girlish admiration in her. I didn't always agree with her taste: She adored Arthur Godfrey, Dwight Eisenhower, and Lawrence Welk. Once my father bought four tickets for my mother and her three unmarried sisters to go to a Liberace concert. They all dressed up for it, as if they hoped the piano player might ask any one of them on a date.

As I listened to Charles repeat the stories I had told him, I thought back to all the times I had dragged my mother to the old Metropolitan Opera House, always hoping I might get her interested, always hoping to see in her some of the excitement I felt. But she went with me to be with me, not to see an opera. My mother never interested herself in anything beyond her children, not even in what interested them.

"Skipper tells me you used to go to see Zinka Milanov," Charles said.

"If he told you so, darling."

I had explained to Charles that Milanov was my favorite

soprano in those days, the early sixties. He had been curious about my license plate, which is ZINKA. She had had such a long career and went on singing for so many years that I named anything I needed to last a long time after her. My old car, bought used, was going to have to go on running until I could afford another. One day, I played my old RCA Victor *Aida*, with Milanov, Jussi Björling, and Leonard Warren, for Charles so that he would understand what I was talking about.

When I was about fifteen, I got it into my head that my mother resembled Zinka Milanov. They were both imposing, big-bosomed women about the same age. Each, in different ways, had thrilled me with her desperate passion. Onstage, at the most dramatic moments, Milanov abandoned herself to her inner music, going far beyond the constraints of decorous acting, throwing herself to the floor, lunging this way and that, clenching her fists to her breast. At home, my mother's overwhelming fear for her children drove her to equally terrifying extremes of melodrama: running from window to window to peek through the blinds if my college-age sister was a few minutes late, holding her hand against her heart as if she might be having an attack, threatening to call the police to report a missing daughter. "Why do you kids treat me like this?" she'd plead. "You know how I worry!"

Now my mother was smiling happily up at Charles, chatting away. How had he managed this? He glanced at me and winked, then turned his full attention back to my mother.

I watched the two of them, remembering how I once cajoled my mother into dressing up as an opera diva. I rifled through her closets and dressers for glamorous garments; stuffed a couch bolster into her bosom; used her mascara, eyebrow pencil, and eye shadow to copy Milanov's distinctive makeup; and got out my Super 8 movie camera. The performance was sort of a spoof of the comedy opera routines that Florence Foster Jenkins was famous for, without sound. I replayed this scene in my mind's eye while my mother chatted with Charles about the operas she certainly had no memory of going to. Anytime I wanted to, I could drop a needle into a groove on my old LPs and still hear Milanov at her peak, but the Super 8 film of my mother was long gone.

"Skipper has told me all about your house in Riverdale," Charles was saying. "You had beautiful peonies in the backyard, didn't you? Do you remember them?"

"Of course, darling."

How I loved those peonies! As a child, I was amazed by how quickly they sprang out of the ground and grew taller each day. I wondered whether, if I just sat quietly on the edge of the flagstone patio, I actually might be able to see them grow. I liked to run my fingers around their fat round buds, like giant green marbles covered with ants, which would soon unfold to huge pink or white or magenta globes of soft, fragile, fragrant petals, the impossible flowers of Chinese scroll paintings. When they were in full bloom, I pressed my face into their silkiness and inhaled their perfume.

"Skipper says he used to bring armloads in for the dining room table."

"Oh, yes, darling." My mother beamed at Charles.

I'd make an arrangement in just the right vase for our table, the peonies with ants still on them, and the ants would crawl over the tablecloth and onto our salty broiled lamb chops and overcooked peas, and then my mother would take the vase off the table. A few fallen petals—magenta, pink, white—would remain around the salt and pepper shakers, and there would always be some ants scurrying out of harm's way. In winter, when the plants along the patio had disappeared beneath the earth, I made fake peonies out of Kleenex, wadding them up around a paper-clip center, then tearing off the edges to imitate the frilled petals, touching my mother's lipstick to them to get just a hint of red, and then unfurling them into big fluffy flowers.

Daydreaming about my childhood, I had no idea how long we'd been sitting at my mother's bedside. I heard Charles say, "Well, I'm glad we've had this chance to talk, Mrs. Wachsberger." He stood and kissed my mother's forehead.

She smiled up at him. "Thank you for coming, darling."

I went to my mother's side. "Mom, do you know who I am?"

"Of course! You're my good friend."

As always, she made me feel desperately sad for her.

On our way out through the long bleak hallway, Charles said, "She knows you're in good hands now."

We got into the car and Charles drove me home.

A few months later my mother died, during the night, alone, at the nursing home. She didn't have to worry about me anymore.

One cold morning Charles sat up suddenly in bed.

"I just dreamed there was a tree right outside our window," he said.

There wasn't one. Our bedroom windows looked out over the flat roof of our kitchen to the south and over the flat roof of our mud porch to the east.

"It was bitterly cold," he went on, "and all the branches were bare. Then a flock of darling little birds landed on all the branches. They started calling to one another, and it was so cold I could see their breath in the air. I worried they would freeze to death. Then suddenly the branches burst into bloom, pink flowers like quince blossoms. It was the warmth of all the little birds' breaths combined that caused the buds to bloom."

"Is that possible?" I asked.

"Anything can happen in a garden."

He went back to sleep.

That spring, Charles and I began to garden together. We were both a little hesitant, in case our egos might clash. Remembering all the years I gardened at other people's homes, Freddie's and Edwin's especially, and how I had always been keenly aware that those gardens were not truly mine, I wanted Charles to feel the Orient garden was his to do with as he pleased. At the same time, the garden was my creation. I had nurtured it for thirteen years from its beginnings in an open field, and I had endless pictures in my mind of what I wanted the garden to become.

One day, I noticed Charles across the garden, perched high on a ladder, pruning the crape myrtle. This was a plant I had learned about only a few years earlier, one day while walking through a Greenport neighborhood. In a backyard there I had seen what looked like a twelve-foot-tall phlox with enormous bright magenta panicles. I asked around and learned it was a young crape myrtle tree. They were not yet widely grown up north. I ordered one with raspberry-pink flowers from a mail-order nursery, and it had grown into a sturdy tree with a dozen tall limbs that each ended in a huge panicle of bright florets in late summer. I loved that tree! I panicked now, seeing limbs and branches falling away this way and that as Charles sawed and clipped. What if cutting it back would prevent it from blooming?

"Honeybun," Charles said before I could speak, "we're going to have a beautiful crape myrtle!"

Without looking at me, he handed down the large limb he had just sawn off, and returned to his pruning. I had to admit (to myself) that the tree looked better already, more compact, more symmetrical.

"I hope you know what you're doing" was all I could come up with.

"Everybody in the South grows crape myrtles, and this is how we prune them down there—*severely*! Each of these limbs will sprout four or five new branches. Wait'll you see how it'll be covered in blooms."

I was doubtful.

"All the trees and shrubs need pruning," Charles said, still snipping away at the crape myrtle. Pruning was something I never had the gumption or guts to do, even though I knew it would be beneficial.

"And there's a lot of weeding to do, too," he went on. *Snip, snip, snip.*

"I like that look in the garden."

"What look? If there's a look here, show it to me, because I cannot find it."

"The laissez-faire look," I said with so little conviction I started to laugh.

"Laissez-faire is all well and good, but the weeds are going to overrun your whole garden, if you let them."

We were both laughing now.

I pictured the garden through Charles's eyes and saw it was out of control. It was that way partly because I liked that wild look, but also because I had become disillusioned doing it all by myself. Even more than that, I had been doing it *for* myself. Now, suddenly, here was Charles, and the garden was *his*, too. He might be working alongside me on a project I'd asked him to help me with, or be off by himself at the other end of the garden, busy at some task he had set for himself.

"Would you hand me the little saw?" he asked, without looking down at me from his ladder, studying the new shape of the crape myrtle. "It's there, under that pile of branches."

As I handed it up to him, seeing him against the brilliant sky, the word *godsend* popped unexpectedly into my mind. I was not brought up in any organized religion. My mother was Protestant, my father was Jewish, but neither practiced. If anything, I was a pagan. I believed that everything in nature—rocks, trees, clouds, birds—had an inner force that could be called upon, summoned to help when needed.

No matter whatever or whoever had sent me Charles, I decided to let go of all those pictures in my mind of what I wanted my garden to be. What difference did it make if Charles was cutting the crape myrtle down to half its size? Charles and I would create new pictures, together. Our garden.

That first May together, Stosh Soito's 'Festiva Maxima' peonies put on a spectacular display. Their short moment of bloom remained a treasured time for me, even as new garden plants grew up around that original clump. They always reminded me of our Riverdale peonies, and of the Kleenex peonies I used to make in the winter. One Sunday afternoon before Charles left for the city, I picked a huge bouquet of the fluffy, fragrant white flowers.

"These are for you to take back to the apartment," I told him.

"Oh, you should have kept them in the garden to enjoy here. I know how much you love peonies."

"They might not last outside until next weekend. The flowers are so fragile that even one rain shower might ruin them." It distressed me to see their huge spoilt flowers lying spattered in mud like roadkill. "This way you can enjoy them

Stosh Soito's peonies put on a spectacular display.

all week. I want you to have a reminder of our garden. Only I've never had much luck bringing bouquets into the city. They get battered on the bus, or go limp, like wet pink lettuce."

"I'll show you how to do it." He carried the peonies to the kitchen, supporting the blossoms the way you would hold a baby's head. "Hand me the cutting board."

He lined up the stems and sliced each one at an angle. "Cut the top off that empty plastic water jug. Then fill it with water." He gathered all the stems into a tight bundle and wedged them into the jug. "Now bring me that sturdy plastic shopping bag. We'll stand it up like this so it can't spill over."

The peonies already perfumed the room with their powdery fragrance. While we waited to leave for the bus, Charles and I made ourselves comfortable on the tapestry couch, looking through a book of famous English gardens to pass the time, turning page after page of ancient stone walls, vine-covered and mossy, worn brick paths weaving through cottage borders, creeping groundcovers greening the interstices of random blue stones, thatched roofs garlanded with climbing roses, massive stone façades espaliered with flowering trees.

"All these houses in England have names," Charles said. "We should have a name for our house, too."

"We do," I said. "It's the Soito house. It will always be the Soito house, for old Mr. Soito, no matter how long we live here."

"No, I mean a name like they have in England, like Hertfordshire House or Chiswick Gardens. What should we call our house? The Wachsberger-Dean House?"

"That doesn't sound very English. How about Adsworthy House," I suggested. "Because we met through an ad."

"Perfect!"

In the car on the way to the bus, Charles, half-hidden by flowers like an exotic Gauguin portrait, said, "I love our peonies from Adsworthy House Gardens!"

We parked at the bus stop and I walked Charles, carrying the huge bouquet, to the bus. That day the hostess, standing at the door and checking off names on the reservation list, was Cleo Tabor, an Orient old-timer.

"Oh, look!" she said to Charles. "Those are Mr. Soito's peonies!"

A Stolen Coleus

Our routine that first summer was for Charles to come to Orient every week on his two days off, which didn't always coincide with my two days off from the nursery. I was selfishly reluctant to give up a weekend in the garden, but it seemed only fair that I should go to the city once in a while for us to have a weekend together there.

"Come have dinner with me one evening at the Carlyle," Charles urged. "I can dine with you when I take my break." After Charles repeated the request a few times during the summer, we finally set a date for a Friday night in the fall.

That Friday I wound up ripping dead pine trees out of a neglected garden in Baiting Hollow, thirty miles west of Orient. This property was perched precariously on the edge of a steep drop above a wild wooded hillside overlooking the Long Island Sound, not so much a garden as a helter-skelter scatter of tough shrubs and indomitable perennials, bayberry and yucca mostly, that could withstand the dry sandy soil and the fierce winter winds, all overgrown with saplings and poison ivy. Black pines had been planted years earlier as a windbreak, but now this type of pine was dying on Long Island from a contagious disease. To get at the dead trees, I had to crawl through misshapen bayberries, cramped on all sides by poison ivy, and then drag the sawn limbs and heavy trunks through underbrush to load them onto the nursery truck.

It was a hot October day and I was drenched in sweat, smeared with pine tar, my face and arms scratched from twigs and pinecones and needles. The work dragged on longer than I had expected. All the while I was afraid of injuring myself or getting poison ivy, not making my bus on time, and not being able to keep my Carlyle date with Charles.

I got to the bus just before it pulled away from the Greenport terminal. I changed out of my work clothes in the tiny bathroom while the bus lurched out of town, then settled into a window seat to watch the North Fork's fall farm views rush past: the long parallel lines of grapes, like olive chenille blankets spread to the horizon, opening onto ochre fields of stubble polka-dotted with pumpkins, switching to tall, rough rows of dried cornstalks.

Landscapes approaching, passing, disappearing, have always inspired me to imagine new adventures ahead. When I was seven, my family traveled by train for the first time to Florida, from Penn Station, overnight in compact compartments with fold-down stainless-steel sinks. I stayed awake in my berth all night, watching the changing landscapes speed past so that I wouldn't miss the first palm tree, a scrubby palmetto somewhere in the Carolinas. Each click-clack of the wheels on the tracks was bringing me closer to my daydreams.

Our Florida hotel had tropical gardens tucked in around every entrance and pathway, enormous odd-colored foliage patterned like batik or tie-dyed fabric, and palm trees: coconut palms, date palms, royal palms, traveler palms. I loved the evocative paper-rustle sounds that breezes make when they set dried palm fronds rubbing against one another. It never occurred to me that these gardens had been designed by someone—or that I could someday design a garden like these myself.

It was still light when the bus pulled up at the familiar Seventy-ninth Street stop. Outside Charles's apartment building, the tree pits he designed were ablaze with exotics: a neon chartreuse-and-magenta coleus, a white-and-red-spotted caladium that he had told me was called 'Miss Muffet', tall orange canna lilies, purple elephant ears, and big, bushy, bronzy clumps of coleus 'Codrington College'—a Florida planting.

I hurried upstairs—I had a set of keys—to scrub off the pine tar, take a quick shower, and dress in a tie and jacket, which Charles had instructed me were required for dinner at the Carlyle. I remembered how all those years ago in our Florida hotel room I couldn't wait to dress in the vacation wardrobe my mother had let me pick out—pink linen trousers, Madras plaid jacket, bow tie, spotless brown-and-white Oxford shoes—to walk around the hotel grounds, ready for whatever romance might befall a seven-year-old, careful to stay out of the bright sun as my mother had warned. From the shade of palm fronds, I watched an athletic young swimmer emerge, glistening, from the turquoise hotel pool, rivulets dripping down his tanned back, down his legs from his yellow swimming trunks, a stripe of untanned skin at his waistband; watched him walk away down a coral-stone path, leaving a trail of damp crescent footprints. I remember placing one of my feet, in its brand-new little Oxford shoe, on the closest of the footprints before it faded. I wanted to follow the trail.

Now, in my jacket and tie, walking the few blocks from Charles's apartment to the Carlyle after working on sandy earth all day, the city pavement was a surprise beneath my feet. The neighborhood streets that I had known so well when my mother lived on Eightieth Street seemed to offer new promises. The whole experience was brand-new. I mused as I walked that Charles referred to *our* garden, *our* country house, *our* apartment, but I still found myself saying *Charles's* apartment. Now I would be seeing Charles in a new setting, his place of work. I was apprehensive. I didn't feel comfortable visiting friends at work. I always worried I was interrupting, or that the boss might not approve.

I pushed through the revolving glass door of the Carlyle into a glamorous lobby. Across the room, Charles, in his tuxedo, was waiting at the entrance to the restaurant. I was stunned by how handsome he looked, with his perfectly tied black bow tie and glimmering studs down the front of his dress shirt.

"Good evening, Mr. Wachsberger!" he welcomed me formally, the way he would a Carlyle regular. I looked at this tall, elegant man as if I were seeing him for the first time. It was turning out that every time I saw Charles, I felt it was for the first time. *Who is this extraordinary person?*

I followed him down a few carpeted steps. "This is the Lower Gallery," he said, gesturing at the elegant oval room, papered in indigo-and-gold wallpaper, punctuated with scenes of what I thought was Venice, each framed in a trompe l'oeil gilt rondelle.

"St. Mark's," I said, hoping to sound like a sophisticated world traveler.

"Everybody thinks it's Venice," he said without giving me the feeling he was correcting me, "but it's based on original paintings of Constantinople. The artist was Italian, which is why it might look like Venice. That isn't St. Mark's. It's Hagia Sofia. This paper was hand-stenciled specifically for this space," he explained. "You could probably do it better!"

Not really, and I hope I never have to do trompe l'oeil again, I thought as I followed his tall, straight tuxedoed back past an enormous floral arrangement that must have been fifteen feet tall and almost as wide.

"This display is changed every week," he commented.

Charles, in his tuxedo, was waiting at the entrance to the restaurant.

That night it was evergreen magnolia leaves, tall spires of orchids, and some dark red tropical exotic thing in a magnificent urn.

I followed him into a larger formal dining room, all the tables draped in white linen and set with candles and small bouquets of yellow roses. "Will this table be acceptable?" he asked, pulling out a chair for me, adjusting it as I sat.

Candlelight glinted off crystal, champagne sparkled into fragile flutes here while cutlery sliced into a roast there, a serving table of desserts wheeled past behind me. I looked around at the tables of elegantly dressed diners quietly conversing, and thought, *No one else here was ripping out dead pine trees three hours ago!*

Charles leaned close. "That's Kitty Carlisle, dining at that table right next to you," he said softly. "Moss Hart's widow."

"I used to watch her on *To Tell the Truth*."

"So did I! Back home in Tennessee, I thought she was the epitome of New York sophistication."

"She looks exactly the same now, forty years later. Her hair is still shiny black."

A waiter set a slender flute of champagne by my plate. Charles introduced me to him while he flourished a menu in a leather binding, unfolded it, and placed it before me. It was exquisitely printed.

"I'll join you in a minute," he said. "By the way, these are original Redoutés." He indicated a row of gilt-framed prints on the walls. "The white flowers from his *Lilies* series." He went off to take care of a customer's needs, gliding smoothly through the dining room as if in a ballet.

I looked at the prints, in case he was going to discuss them. White lilies, white hosta flowers. I was more familiar with Redouté's *Les Roses*. Then I looked at the prices on the menu and my heart skipped a beat. Charles had told me my meal would go on his tab, at half price, but I was unnerved nevertheless. I was not used to elegant New York nightspots and hoped I wouldn't embarrass myself—or worse, embarrass Charles—by acting gauche.

When I was five and six and seven I used to watch *The Stork Club* on CBS television every weeknight, Sherman Billingsley visiting over cocktails with whichever celebrities happened to be in town. It was all very glamorous. That was where I wanted to be, not in front of the grainy-screened, black-and-white TV in my middle-class Riverdale home. It did not seem possible then that I'd ever get to dine anywhere like the Stork Club.

"Does anything appeal to you?" Charles asked, back again, standing next to me.

"What do you suggest?" I was playing it safe.

"The Dover sole is our specialty. We have it flown over from England every day."

It was forty-five dollars, the most expensive item on the menu.

"It's what I'm having," Charles continued. "If you don't like it you can send it back and have something else."

"I'll have the Dover sole." I felt giddy. "I came here once to see Bobby Short. I think it was after my high school prom."

"Oh, Bobby's still here!" he said. "His thirtieth anniversary is coming up in a couple of years. My mother sends him a jar of her homemade fig jam every Christmas. She has a huge fig tree next to her house. She came up to hear him perform once, and he sang a special song for her. I adore Bobby! Will you have white wine with the sole, or do you want to continue with champagne?"

A waiter placed a small plate in front of me on which was arranged a cone of creamy rice smothered with pale ivory shavings, saying, "Compliments of the Carlyle." A warm, pungent aroma wafted up.

"White truffle risotto," Charles explained. "You'll like

it." He handed the waiter the larger of the wineglasses already on the table. "I think white with the sole," he said to the waiter, then to me, "I'll bring you a wine list." Before I could say, "You order, I'm not a wine connoisseur," he was needed across the room. "Go ahead and eat your risotto before it gets cold," he said, disappearing behind me, leaving me alone with the crystal and candlelight.

I sampled a forkful of risotto, the paper-thin shavings of white truffle redolent of walks through damp, ferny woods.

This was not the first time I'd had white truffles. Miraculously, starting when I was ten, a madcap heiress saved me, in classic screwball-comedy fashion, from a life of boring conventionality. It was the winter I was reading and rereading and quoting lines from the currently best-selling *Auntie Mame* to anyone who would listen, and wishing my life were as exciting as Little Patrick's, Mame's nephew. One snow-bright day our front doorbell rang and I happened to be the one to open the door. Before me stood a tall, slender young woman in a mink coat, shielding her mouth with one hand. Over her shoulder, I saw a powder blue Mercedes convertible sports car parked behind a snow pile at the end of our front path, top down.

"I'm having an allergic reaction to soft-shell crabs," she whispered the way Marilyn Monroe spoke in movies. "I can't take my hand away because my upper lip has swollen to five times its normal size. I look like a Ubangi."

I knew what a Ubangi looked like from my beloved *National Geographic* magazines. I didn't know or care what soft-shell crabs were.

This was Iris Love, my sister's friend from the Institute of Fine Arts, where they were each studying classical Greek and Roman art history. I had heard Freddie speak of Iris, but the name had only conjured up for me a clump of bronzy-

purple flowers growing near a pond in our Riverdale neighborhood. I loved those almost-brown flowers, so unlike any
others I'd ever seen. Now my sister bounded down our stairs
with her ski things, and I was instantly jealous that she had
such an intriguing friend who was going to take her away,
without me.

We maneuvered Iris out of her fur coat so that she never
had to remove her hand from her lip, and led her to our
kitchen, which suddenly looked to me as dreary as the kitchen
in *The Honeymooners*. Iris seemed to speak Italian, French,
Greek, and German with equal authority, at least as far as I
could tell. She told alluring stories about her travels around
Europe, spiced with foreign words in appropriate accents, like
clues in a treasure hunt.

She explained that she was named after the ancient Greek
goddess of the rainbow, messenger to the gods on Mount
Olympus, and at that moment it did seem to me that a rainbow
had landed in our kitchen, right there amid our persimmon
vinyl seat cushions and blue-and-white Colonial-scene wallpaper. Within a few minutes, Iris promised me an invitation
to her great-aunt Peggy Guggenheim's palazzo in Venice. I
had no idea who she was talking about or what it all meant,
beyond the gondolas and dark, handsome Italians I had seen
in movies like *Three Coins in the Fountain* and *Summertime*,
but I was ready to go. Just let me grab my baby blanket.

Iris became my very own Auntie Mame. She took me to
the old Metropolitan Opera House to see the great singers of
the 1950s and '60s, Renata Tebaldi, Jussi Björling, Leonard
Warren, and Zinka Milanov, with dinners before at '21' or
The Forum of the Twelve Caesars or, my favorite, Trader Vic's,
a Polynesian restaurant decorated with fake palm trees, where
Iris always charmed the waiters into letting me drink an al-
coholic concoction that came with a real gardenia floating on

top, which I wanted more than the drink. Gardenia to this day remains my favorite floral fragrance. After the opera, there were suppers of fondue and Châteauneuf-du-Pape or Lacryma Christi, which Iris explained meant tears of Christ, made from grapes grown on the slopes of Mount Vesuvius.

One crisp fall night, explaining it was *the season*, she ordered fettuccini with white truffles for us, of course ordering it in Italian, *"al tartufo bianco."* The waiter brought what to me looked like a dried horse chestnut seedpod to the table and scraped the peculiar thing over a grater, so that thin slices wafted down onto our piles of pasta. I knew from Iris's murmurs that the aroma was supposed to be delicious, but to me it smelled like gym socks.

I finished my Carlyle *risotto al tartufo bianco*, which by this point in my life I'd acquired a taste for. I was thinking about what needed doing in the garden, what chores I might accomplish if I weren't in the city, and how they would have to wait until I was back in Orient, when a waiter brought the Dover sole. The fragrance of lemon and melted butter, warm as candlelight, called me back from my imagined garden. Charles returned and settled in across from me, his narrow bow tie and diamond dress-shirt studs making him look as debonair as a leading man in a thirties romantic comedy, the same Charles I had gotten used to seeing in his weekend gardening outfit of torn, muddy work clothes, muck boots, and floppy sun hat.

"Do you like the sole?"

I tasted a forkful, a cloud of butter, and washed it down with white wine.

Before I could answer, Charles rose suddenly. Kitty Carlisle and her party were getting ready to leave. Charles lifted the black beaded jacket she had draped over the back of her chair, helped her into it, and escorted her to the steps leading out of the Lower Gallery.

"I wish I could have told her how much I enjoyed her on *To Tell the Truth*," I said, when Charles returned.

"I'm sure she would have appreciated it. She's very gracious."

"I would have felt awkward. I'm not used to places like this." I told him about Iris, and the fine restaurants she took me to when I was a young teenager.

"You're more sophisticated than I am," he said. "I was a hick in Tennessee when you were going to the opera with your Auntie Mame."

"But when Iris took me to all those chic Manhattan nightspots, I was there only on her whim. I could never go on my own. I always felt like I was on the outside looking in. When I grew up, I couldn't afford those places."

Seeing Charles seated across from me in his tuxedo—*who is this person?*—my date, my partner, I finally felt I belonged in an elegant restaurant.

"Your Auntie Mame was in recently," he said. Charles knew Iris only by sight, since she occasionally dined at the Carlyle. "She and her companion were inspecting a huge ancient Greek vase."

"I can just picture that."

I had been present at so many similar scenes: Iris, in a nubby Chanel suit, pushing aside the tableware and crystal glasses to make room for a rare, perfectly intact black-figured kylix or lekythos, then licking the tip of her index finger, pressing the moisture onto the vase's surface, bringing the wet spot close to her nose, dramatically sniffing the damp clay for the aroma of authenticity, then widening her eyes, either with approval or with triumph at spotting a fake.

"Iris was kind of my deus ex machina," I told Charles. "When I got a little older, she invited me to wild parties. I remember, once, Andy Warhol dropped by dressed as a 1940s gangster; I think he even had a fake machine gun—I guess it must have been fake. The women wore blazers and men's ties, which shocked me back then in the sixties. One time Franco Zeffirelli asked me to have dinner. I didn't go, though. All my mother's warnings against strangers. I was afraid to go with him."

"Good! Because if you had, then we might not ever have met."

I was thinking, *But maybe I'd have been in a Zeffirelli film!* "I saw Iris not long after I met you," I told Charles. "I was finally able to tell my Auntie Mame that I had found someone special."

"Did she approve?"

"She said, 'Ah, then Aphrodite, the goddess of love, has finally smiled upon you,'" in that breathy way she speaks, and I said, 'Yes, but it took fifty years. Half a century!' and she said, 'Well, Skipper, what's half a century to Aphrodite?'"

When Charles could finally leave for the night, we walked home together to *our* apartment. The evening was mild, the sky fall-clear. We stopped to admire Charles's tree-pit gardens, at their lush late-season peak. But something was very wrong: there were only holes where the neon-colored coleus and polka-dotted caladiums had been when I set off for the Carlyle earlier that evening.

"They've been yanked out with their roots!" Charles said. His tall frame turned rigid next to me as he became ominously quiet.

"I'm so sorry," I said, helplessly.

"We'll just go tomorrow and buy some more," is all he said. But I knew it wasn't okay.

The thefts continued, night after night, whenever the doorman was away from his post. Charles would replace a stolen plant, then that new one would vanish. He would call me in Orient to report which plant had been stolen this time.

"They took the purple elephant ears tonight!"

Another night the orange cannas disappeared.

"Honeybun, 'Codrington College' is gone!"

"Someone with very good taste is creating a fabulous garden somewhere else."

Charles got more and more upset, and frustrated. It saddened me to see him so hurt, after all the love he put into those gardens. I couldn't bear that some stranger was causing him so much pain. I tried to come up with helpful suggestions.

"How about if we stretched wire mesh over the plants?"

"No, if we were going to have an ugly garden, why bother?"

The next time I was in the city, I helped him make cardboard signs, saying: ENOUGH IS ENOUGH! LEAVE SOMETHING FOR YOUR NEIGHBORS TO ENJOY! But the thief was insatiable.

"Well, if they're going to keep stealing our plants, then I'm not going to grow them anymore. I'll just put in ivy like everyone else."

That was an idle threat. Charles would not do *anything* like everyone else.

"It isn't sunny enough for tropical plants, anyway," he rationalized. "I've taken such good care of the locust trees, they've grown so large now that they shade the gardens completely."

"Why not create shade gardens, then?" I suggested. "We could make it look like a tiny bit of woodland under each of the trees."

"Honeybun, that's a fabulous idea!"

"And let's take the tropicals out to Orient."

We replaced the tropicals with evergreen groundcovers

so that there would be winter interest as well as summer display: liriope for their tufts of straplike leaves and fall berries after sprays of lavender flowers, epimedium for shiny foliage dancing atop wiry stems and pale yellow spurred springtime flowers, heuchera 'Autumn Bride' for its long-lasting sprays of white flowers in autumn, *Rohdea japonica* for a bold winter presence of wide leathery leaves. We planted mahonia and butcher's broom, small evergreen shrubs, all good shade plants, hoping that they would not be showy enough to attract thieves. We tucked grape hyacinth and miniature daffodils into spaces between the perennials, for spring color.

For height, we planted a climbing hydrangea at the base of each tree. We knew the hydrangeas would be slow to climb, but their lush foliage and panicles of ivory flowers would be worth the wait. As the trees' canopies grew, the tree pits would evolve into dappled micro-woodlands.

The thefts stopped. Charles perked up.

In Orient, we settled the tropicals into the sunniest spots of our garden, safe for what remained of their short summer lives. At a yard sale, I found six almost-brand-new pink plastic flamingos—just in time, because the person behind me was aggressively reaching for them. Tropical gardening was becoming hot! I whisked the flamingos back to our garden, where we set them among the cannas and coleus and gingers, and now I had my little Florida garden, Zone 7 in drag as Zone 9.

Passionflowers and Bindweed

Under my laissez-faire gardening, anything that thrived and prospered won my heart, even if its vigor threatened nearby plants. When a sturdy new shoot popped up unexpectedly, I tended to leave it where it was and watched to see how it fit into the picture. Charles, though, liked to make sure that each plant had its own space. He ripped out any one that might smother another. I knew he was right, of course.

When he complained about my placing a tender young rose too close to larger bushes, I reminded him, "Survival of the fittest."

"Survival of the fittest is all well and good," he retorted, "but if you put a mouse into the same cage with an elephant, no matter how fit the mouse is, if the elephant steps on it, that's it for the mouse."

I've killed a lot of plants over the years. It's true I planted some too closely, but others were from hot climates that perished because they weren't hardy in our growing zone, which I knew might be the case when I planted them. I tried anyway, believing I could *will* them to survive the Orient winter.

Other plants died because I introduced a few mass murderers into the garden, invasive weeds that choke out everything in their path. When I first started the garden, I found what I thought was a wild morning glory twining around a fence post near the outhouse. The pale pink flowers were pretty in a modest way, certainly appropriate to a cottage garden. The vine even looked like it might be perennial. What a find! A perennial morning glory! I wouldn't have to start 'Heavenly Blue' from seed every spring. And so I left it growing there by the fence.

That's how I learned about bindweed, the most invasive weed in our garden. Its roots spread underground, crisscrossing like a map of the New York subway system, and it pops up in gangs of tough stranglers ready to race each other to the top of the nearest stem or stalk, twisting so tightly that if you try to pull the bindweed off it will take the victim out of the ground along with it. Richard Iverson, the horticultural expert at Farmingdale and Charles's longtime friend, told us when he first visited that we'd have to dig up the entire garden and spray the bare earth with Roundup. I don't use herbicides, and I had no intention of digging up a single plant. Instead, Charles patiently and systematically set about unwinding the bindweed from thorny roses, fragile lily stems, and dense shrubs, so that when he ripped the weed out by its roots he wouldn't snap off a stem or a branch from the victim plant along with it.

I loved watching him march into the thick of it, tall in his muck boots, determined to get out every last bit of bindweed.

"You must be digilant," he would say, which, because I was already familiar with Charles's slight dyslexia, I understood to mean vigilant . . . or diligent . . . or both. Even if he started on another task, pretty soon he'd be knee-deep in a pile of wrenched bindweed vines, unwinding just one more.

"This is a tricky one," he'd say when I called him to lunch. "Look how it's imitating this other plant, so it can try to get in here without my noticing it!" And then he'd spend another half hour unwinding it. Next time I called, the soup getting cold, I'd see him wheeling a barrow piled high with bindweed to the compost.

"I'll show them 'survival of the fittest!' " he'd say, finally sitting down to lunch.

My passionflower vines posed a different problem. Even though this is an incredibly invasive plant, I didn't want Charles to pull out every last vine, because passionflowers and I have a long, entwined history ourselves.

I first saw passionflowers the summer I was nine, when my parents took me to Bermuda for a week's vacation. It was the most exotic place I had ever been, even more intriguing than Florida. Pastel cottages with red tile roofs nestled under banana leaves, surrounded by palm groves, and in the sun-drenched distance a turquoise sea sparkled inside pink coral reefs. Best of all, the gardens were lushly tropical without any danger of snakes, unlike Florida. I could wander right into the densest palmetto patch. Only the bright green little lizards startled me, darting in every direction like shards of glass from a shattered bottle. On the grounds of the Castle Harbor Hotel an old black man in a tattered straw hat taught me, with a lilting accent, how to catch the little lizards. First he plucked a long blade of grass, then twisted it into a miniature lasso. He quietly, stealthily, and gently slipped this over an unsuspecting lizard's head and tightened it lightly around its neck. All that was required was patience. Soon I could actually hold the tiny creatures in my hand before letting them go. The male lizards sometimes put on a threatening show, puffing up their bright red throats to twice their size. I daydreamed about those lizards forever after, but of course they would not survive in our Riverdale yard.

We visited a Bermuda perfume factory, where the major product was passionflower perfume. We were each given a fresh-picked passionflower wrapped in cellophane, reminding me of my sister's prom corsage. It was not like any flower I had ever imagined, resembling more an elaborate structure blown from glass: Alternating lilac and white petals formed a platter under a bowl of frilly filaments banded purple-mauve-white, like the tentacles of a sea urchin, and out of the center of this amazing assemblage protruded a complicated column of stamens and sepals. This was the blue passionflower, *Passiflora caerulea*. Its evocative fragrance was to haunt my memories.

I carried the souvenir passionflower in its cellophane wrapping on my lap on the plane home, and tried to keep it fresh long past any flower's natural life span. It was a shriveled brown thing by the time I threw it out.

Back in Riverdale, I read everything I could about passionflowers. I was disappointed to learn that the name did not refer to romance or carnal lust, but to the Passion of Christ. The early Spanish invaders of the New World were intrigued by this flower and, striving as they did to see Christ in every new discovery, identified the complex parts of the flower as allegories: the pistils represented the Three Nails, the stamens were the Five Wounds, the circle of filaments were the Crown of Thorns, and the petals and sepals the Apostles.

I was nine, I was a romantic, and I had no interest in Scripture. I just wished that this exotic flower could survive in Riverdale.

I tried to grow the blue passionflower as a potted houseplant, at different times in different homes, never with luck. One summer after I'd begun the garden in Orient, I read in a mail-order plant catalogue that *Passiflora incarnata*, or maypop, whose flowers look very much like those of the blue passionflower, was "marginally hardy" here in Zone 7. I ordered one. A spindly slip of a vine arrived in the mail. I planted it against the south-facing wall of the garage and hoped that it would survive. It did live through that first winter and grew into a modest vine at one corner of the garage, nothing like the blankets of passionflowers smothering pastel cottages that I remembered from Bermuda. The following spring it began to spread. And spread. It turned out to be as invasive as bindweed, only much, much taller. In a season it climbs thirty feet into trees, not by twining like bindweed, but by reaching out with threadlike tendrils and grabbing hold. I have watched these tendrils wave back and forth in the air, like the feelers of a praying mantis, searching for something to grab on to. Once they find something—anything—they coil tightly around it and pull themselves closer. The vines come up throughout the entire garden now. They can't harm a sturdy shrub or tree, but they can smother smaller plants— rosebushes, in particular—by shading them with their abundant foliage.

"It's a weed in Tennessee," Charles told me. His childhood experience with passionflower did not evoke either romance or exotica. "I used to rip it out of our backyard."

He took on the job of keeping it under control, yanking it out wherever it sprung up, except where I asked him to allow it to festoon a stand of witch hazels with swags of summer color, pouring its intoxicating perfume into the humid air.

"I know you love your passionflowers," he'd say, eyeing the patch with annoyance as he walked past. If it were up to him, the vines would be gone from the garden altogether.

It's not just their beauty that endears them to me, but precisely that vigorous aggressiveness that is a threat to the garden. I admire anything that thrives if it's not supposed to be hardy. If it has gone so far as to elbow its way to the forefront and shows off unashamedly, it wins my heart. I don't like to rip out anything so determined to have its way.

I like to think I am "determined" myself—it's a quality I admire in people as well as in plants—but "stubborn" is how some people describe me. I grew up surrounded by large, formidable women—my mother and her sisters. I survived in their shadows, but I was determined to find my own sun. Once, I sneaked out of our Riverdale backyard and ran off to the empty wooded lot near my school, P.S. 181. Speckled violets grew there, and each spring I'd look longingly at the woods from my classroom window. Violets in bloom meant that the end of the school term was not far off. Who knew what else might grow in those woods? I'd seen pictures of all sorts of woodland plants, tiny things hidden under fallen logs, spotted like salamanders, delicate as orchids, rare as emeralds. The woods were only a block deep, and there was no chance of getting lost, so I had ventured into the most secluded, shadiest, woodsiest part to search for violets when I heard my mother shrieking from the sidewalk, "Skipper! Oh my God, where are you?" She'd discovered I was missing from our backyard, but I don't know how she knew where I'd gone. She was kind of psychic that way. I heard the underbrush crackle beneath her feet as she stalked into the lot, screaming my name, pulling branches apart before her like King Kong searching for Fay Wray, and then she appeared between two saplings, glasses askew, hair disheveled and full of twigs, her face scratched, her stockings torn, which made her panicked appearance all the more terrifying. I had to go home with her. She wasn't interested in staying to look for violets.

In the Orient garden, I have let wild violets spread wherever they wish. There are thousands: purple, white, white speckled with blue, even a rosy pink. One that I actually bought (I have lost the variety name) blooms earlier than all the others, in late winter, with dark purple flowers so intensely fragrant that a vase of one tiny flower on its thread-like stem is a sufficient table decoration. Violets can grow into a mat so dense that nothing will break through, so I do need to keep them away from tender young plants. But they are the perfect groundcover under shrubs and trees, choking out weeds. And they remind me of my school days at P.S. 181.

Charles loves them, too, and doesn't mind their aggressiveness. They are small and easy to rip out, and therefore harmless. But when I decided I wanted bamboo in the Orient garden, Charles reminded me about the bindweed and passionflowers.

"This is a nonrunning variety," I explained. "*Phyllostachys nigra*. The catalogue says it's a clumper. And the canes mature to a dark purple."

He was not impressed. "Go ahead, if you want purple all over your garden."

The first three years it stayed where I planted it, seducing me with its graceful swaying in the slightest breeze. Its bright chartreuse leaves turned out to be evergreen here, beautiful against the dark canes. Then one spring morning when I checked out the garden I was astonished by what looked like hundreds of javelins poking up out of all the beds, as if hurled there by some invading army. It was the bamboo emerging, ready to march to victory. It ate up a third of the garden that year.

We set to digging out the underground runners, thick and muscular as a man's arm. Charles refrained from saying he had warned me, but his expression as he dug and pulled and sawed said it all.

"So much for *clumping* bamboo," was his sotto voce remark.

I reluctantly began to realize I should listen to Charles, but I still could not resist trying dangerous plants. Charles warned me to rip out all the *Clerodendron bungei* as soon as he saw it coming up in beds far from where I had planted it, but I didn't. I loved its flowers the size of softballs formed of thousands of tiny magenta florets, and its sweet and summery perfume. It looked so exotic in the catalogue photos that I couldn't believe it would be hardy, or else why wouldn't it be in every garden? Well, there are good reasons why it is not in every garden. For one, the foliage stinks. But the main reason no one grows it is that it will choke out every other plant in its path. I'm still ripping it out, which is an especially onerous chore because the stems and leaves smell so awful. Charles doesn't say, "I told you so," but he leaves this one for me to deal with.

The Basjoo bananas, too, have proven more aggressive than I would have expected. This variety of banana tree is sometimes called the Japanese fiber banana, and it is hardy in the north. It dies to the ground each winter, in the same way a peony does, and then with the spring warmth new stalks emerge. Huge banana leaves unfurl from the centers of the stalks, looking like giant cigars at first, until they spiral open into six-foot-long leaves. By late summer, the banana trees are twenty feet tall. If a long, hot summer follows a mild winter, the trees might set fruit, amazing to watch. The flower starts off looking like a purple artichoke on the end of a flexible gooseneck lamp. As the flower grows, its petals peel back and tiny bananas emerge from beneath each one. At maturity, the pendant ball of fruit is the size of a street lamp. The bananas are not edible; the plant is grown in Asia for the fine fibers extracted from its pith, used to make gossamer fabrics.

I planted two small stalks, one alongside the garage, another near a Virginia magnolia. Where there was one stalk, there were soon twenty, in groves stretching eight feet across.

The grove near the Virginia magnolia shaded it so much that it made the tree grow into a distorted shape. Charles began to remove the "pups," as the new banana shoots are called, from around the perimeter so that the grove would not spread any further. Finally, we dug up that entire clump. We've been giving away young banana trees to whoever wants them ever since.

Little by little we are ridding the garden of plants that won't stay put. But I originally chose these plants because they are intriguing in some way or other, and I can't bear to lose them altogether. Charles rips them out and I replant them in the wild bed at the eastern edge of the property, at the foot of a woods that has grown up in the adjacent field. Here now are clumps of ironweed, joe-pye weed, a stand of the *Clerodendron bungei*, rice-paper plant, tansy, and mint. I keep moving passionflowers here, too, trying to get them to establish themselves so that we can eradicate them from the rest of the garden, but they don't take.

It's become a running joke. When Charles sees me ordering a new plant from a catalogue, he asks, "Where are you going to find room for that?" and I answer innocently, "In front of the woods."

Sometimes Charles orders a plant for me that even I had decided was too extravagant. When I was creating my faux Florida garden, he surprised me with a gift of a rare variegated canna 'Stuttgart', its big pointed leaves striped and slashed green-gray-white. I knew he'd spent one hundred dollars on one tuber, because I had been coveting it from its photos in garden magazines. It turned out to be a weak grower, and its leaves burned in the sunlight, the white turning an ugly brown like stained china. It was a mess. I didn't say anything negative about it to Charles because he had been so happy to be able to give me something he knew I wanted, but

I could tell from the way he looked at it that he hated it as much as I did. When one day he finally said, "I'm ripping it out," and added that it had been a waste of money, mumbling something about false advertising, I was much relieved.

Canna 'Stuttgart' wound up on the compost heap.

It wasn't the only exorbitantly expensive plant gift Charles lavished on me. Once he presented me with a small box shipped from a peony nursery, beaming, anticipating my pleasure.

"It's a rare tree peony called 'Companion of Serenity'," he told me, and I think the name appealed to him as much as the huge, pale pink, flamboyant flowers with petals as delicate as sheer Chinese silk that he showed me in the catalogue photo. I eagerly unpacked the plant. For an undisclosed (but I'm sure large) sum of money, we had received a tiny tuber sprouting a two-inch stem with one limp leaf. Charles was dismayed.

"We might as well throw it out right now," he said.

"No! I'll take good care of it. It will grow."

"Go for it," he said, without conviction, and went back to ripping out bindweed.

I felt bad that he was disappointed. I knew he had wanted me to be thrilled with his gift, and I was determined to nurture the miserable little thing to perfect health, and grow it on to blossom for us, however many years it might take. I dug a large hole and filled it with a mixture of our compost and carefully worked soil, and I set a metal cage around the tiny plant so that no one would step on it. Charles did not have faith it would prosper, but I knew it would. Sometimes I can just tell. It did live, but it would be four years before it bloomed.

One thing that was worrying me that first summer was that Charles's two days off were spent gardening, and I felt he should not have to work all day in the garden after working all week at the restaurant, just because I wanted to.

So I was glad when he began photographing the garden while I weeded and planted and reorganized. He claimed he was a beginner photographer, but his portraits of flowers and foliage and his landscape shots of the garden were breathtaking. With the same unerring eye for color and composition that guided him to amass his unique collection of abstract expressionist prints, he composed exquisite views of our garden. In his photographs, I saw my own dreams of the garden realized. Seeing *my* garden through Charles's eyes made me understand more than anything that it was now *ours*.

I began painting watercolors based on Charles's photographs, especially ones that included friends visiting the garden, because I like to paint portraits. Charles's new photographs inspired me to produce a series of watercolors based on old family photographs that would, all together, constitute a kind of autobiography. I set about that task, searching out old snapshots in albums. The project was to become my most compelling artistic endeavor.

Also that first summer, Freddie, who was president of the Oysterponds Historical Society, invited Charles to exhibit his collection of prints at the society's museum. The exhibition would be a year in the planning, during which time I began to understand how deeply involved Charles was in his collection. Charles, ever gracious, did refer to his collection as *ours*, as I referred to *our* garden, but I had had nothing to do with the assembling of the prints. I had worked on the garden before we met, as long as Charles had worked on his collection, but unlike Charles's participation in the garden—his additions, his editing, his careful pruning, his photographs, his total involvement—I was not knowledgeable enough to add anything to the collection of prints, or to alter it, and I averred from the beginning that this was Charles's creation alone.

At that time, the collection consisted of thirty-eight prints. Not all were framed, so Charles set about having them framed over the winter, a few at a time, whenever he could afford it. Only the finest framer in New York came up to Charles's standards, so it was a great expense, but he was looking forward to sharing the works, and even just to seeing them all hung together in one space.

The museum building was the old Orient Schoolhouse, a small one-room clapboard structure. Close to the opening date of Charles's show, the previous exhibition was still hanging. Courtney, the overworked museum curator, didn't think that was a problem, but it worried Charles. Courtney's handsome, apple-cheeked face and reassuring smile had no effect on him.

"He doesn't understand how important these prints are," Charles complained one evening, close to sobbing. "He keeps promising me he'll have the walls up and ready in time to hang the show, but the opening is three days away."

That evening, he went to the schoolhouse after dinner to help move things along. He did not come back until after midnight, by which time I was petrified that something terrible had happened. I heard him come in, but he didn't come upstairs to bed. I listened to him stomping around downstairs. *He's murdered Courtney!* I decided. Would I hide him from the police? Would I help him escape by ferry to Connecticut? Eventually he came to bed, emotionally drained.

"It's still not ready," he gasped. "I want to call Charlotte!"

Charlotte Hanson had taken over as president of the historical society that summer, when Freddie's term ended.

"You can't call Charlotte at two in the morning!"

We didn't sleep. "What time is it?" he kept asking. At five, Charles said, "I'm calling her now."

"You've got to wait at least until seven!"

I could get him to wait only until precisely six, when he

sat down on the top step of the bedroom stairs, dialed Charlotte's number, and began sobbing before she even answered the phone. I sat next to him and held him tight as he tried to speak through his sobs. He managed to get the story out, gasping for breath between each word, his shoulders heaving as I held on to him.

"If they don't have the place ready," he told her, one painful word at a time, "I'll withdraw the collection. Just say I've become ill and have had to cancel the exhibition."

This broke my heart. All the pieces had been framed, he'd written catalogue notes for each piece, and wall notes as well. He'd sent invitations to all his friends, to curators, to print dealers, to gallery owners, and to all the artists still living who were represented in the collection.

After that phone call, Charles collapsed onto the bed in a stupor. I had never seen him like this before. The only thing I could think of was to call his sister Frieda in Chicago and ask what I should do.

"Get him some peach ice cream," she said, sounding more like she was in Georgia than Illinois.

Okay, I thought, *whatever*, and I hurried down Village Lane to our Country Store, not at all confident because the selection of Häagen-Dazs there was usually limited.

"You don't by any chance have peach ice cream?" I asked the young man behind the counter, the owner's son.

"We just made some this morning," he said brightly. "This summer, we're going to be making our own ice cream, and peach is our first."

I rushed home with a container, scooped two balls into a bowl, and carried it upstairs to Charles. He raised his head barely enough to swallow a mouthful. Then he propped himself on one elbow to eat a bit more. In a few minutes he was sitting up. He finished the ice cream.

"Delicious, Honeybun! Thank you! Mother always made us peach ice cream every summer."

He hurried to the schoolhouse to continue the preparations, where he found that Charlotte had rallied all the able-bodied members of the historical society to pitch in. Walls went up, paint was applied, lighting was adjusted, hydrangeas were pruned at the entrance.

The exhibition opened on time. The old schoolhouse's one-room interior had been divided by a T-shaped partition, providing ample wall space to hang each print to advantage and gracefully spotlight it. There was an elegant opening party on the greensward in front of the schoolhouse, attended by the museum members, many of the friends Charles had invited, local artists, and Orient old-timers (who proved surprisingly fascinated by the work, which we had worried might not be of interest to them).

At the gathering, Courtney's wife came over to me and whispered, "You know, the other night, I was afraid Courtney had murdered Charles!"

"And I thought Charles had murdered Courtney!"

Charles and Courtney were all smiles now, but I knew Charles's memory was long.

Later that summer, I was chatting at the nursery with a regular customer who lived in East Marion, the town just west of Orient, and it came up that she was a curator at the Museum of Modern Art, which I hadn't known from previous conversations, so I mentioned Charles's exhibit and asked if she had by any chance seen it.

"He's *your* partner?" she exclaimed. "I have to tell you, when I saw the announcement for the show in the local paper, I said to my friend who was visiting, 'Look at this, an exhibition of American abstract expressionist prints at the Oysterponds Historical Society! That'll be a hoot!' And then we

The exhibition opened on time.

went, expecting it to be a joke, and I was flabbergasted. These were the real things, and the finest examples, too! I walked around with my jaw dropped. I mean, Nevelson, and Margo, and Hofmann, and Hartigan." She rattled off the more famous artists. "He's *your* friend?"

I was so proud of Charles. I couldn't wait to tell him that story.

But for Charles, the most wonderful moment came when Courtney told him that the Library of Congress had requested the brochure and checklist of the exhibition for their archives.

"I guess now he understands," Charles said.

I didn't tell Charles that now *I* finally understood what the collection meant to him.

Edwin's comment was perfect: "Skip," he said, "when you first met Charles and he told you he was a collector, you didn't know what he *really* meant. And when you told him you were a gardener, he didn't know what you *really* meant!"

Hummingbirds

We have a framed photograph that I took of Charles with his arm around his mother's shoulders, in front of our climbing rose 'New Dawn', a backdrop of hundreds of disheveled shell pink blossoms. Mother and son are both squinting into bright sunlight, Charles a full head taller. The photograph was taken on Evelyn's seventy-fifth birthday, June 14, 1996, when she had come up from Augusta, Georgia, to celebrate with us. I painted a watercolor based on the photo, and we keep it in the city apartment, to remind us of Evelyn's only visit to our garden.

Orient that week in June was redolent of beach roses and honeysuckle, their commingled fragrances carried on salt-water breezes from the Sound and the bays. Flocks-of-sheep clouds gathered in blue skies, nights were starry above shrubbery studded with the lazy rhythm of fireflies. Our antique roses were at peak bloom.

"Perfect for Mother's first visit." Charles wanted her to see how happy he was with me in Orient.

I had met Evelyn already, in Atlanta when Charles and I went to hear Martile sing Leonora in *Il Trovatore*. We stayed with Bill and his wife, Ginger, and their five children. On the plane, Charles prepared me for meeting them. He told me that Ginger's brother was also named Charles and that his middle name was also Randall, as was Charles's. I wondered about the odds of Charles's brother marrying a woman whose brother had the same first and middle names as his own brother.

"So your brother Bill has a brother named Charles Randall, a brother-in-law named Charles Randall, and his five kids have *two* Uncle Charles Randalls?"

"And not only that. Their other Uncle Charles Randall is gay, too!"

"That must be a challenge for Mormon kids," I said, somewhere over Maryland. Now I began to worry how, as a gay couple, we could be accepted by Mormons. "Why did your brother become a Mormon, anyway?" Charles and I had known each other only a few months. I was still learning about his family, and learning that when Charles was enthused or nervous he talked rapidly, nonstop, in a monologue.

"My father was abusive and he drank too much," Charles said matter-of-factly. "He was an ex-Marine. Everyone else in his battalion was killed right in front of him on the shore in Okinawa. He came out of the war and went directly into a mental hospital. I think they released him too soon. Frieda was in and out of mental institutions, too, while Bill was still in high school. She was diagnosed as schizophrenic."

I am a nervous flyer, so I found it relaxing to listen to Charles talk on and on about his family. I didn't have to try to fit a word in edgewise, not that I'd have been able to.

"My other sister, Angel, had become a Jesus freak and tried to get me to accept Jesus," Charles went on, "because otherwise I was going to burn in hell. I had long hair in those days and had gotten arrested at an anti-Nixon protest. I got arrested a few times, actually. Then we had to check Frieda into Highland; that's the mental hospital in Asheville, North Carolina, where Zelda Fitzgerald was killed when it burned down. Frieda was getting shock treatments there. She got twelve of them altogether. I guess my brother Bill just looked at what was going on with the rest of us and decided it was safer to be a Mormon."

Thousands of feet below, farm-quilted, cloud-speckled Georgia was rising up to meet us.

"My parents divorced in 1971," Charles continued, "when I was twenty-two. Mother didn't want the divorce, even though my father was a mess. She was going through menopause at the same time, and she'd been through Frieda's mental problems, my being gay and having long hair, Angel's forays into religious fanaticism, and Bill's conversion to Mormonism. She said to me, 'If one more thing goes wrong, *I'm* having a nervous breakdown! It's *my* turn now!' But she survived it all. Somehow."

I could not imagine my own mother surviving all that. I could hear her lamenting, *Why are you kids doing this to me? Do you want to kill me?*

"When my brother got married," Charles went on, his slight drawl getting stronger the nearer we got to Atlanta, "Mother went to the reception . . . of course we couldn't go to his wedding, Mormons don't allow non-Mormons at weddings . . . and my father was there with his second wife, and my mother went up to her and said, 'I hope you have better luck with him than I did.' Mother never remarried. She said once was enough for her. Then, when my father was getting divorced from his new wife, he had a heart attack and died on the day he was supposed to sign the divorce papers, on his way to the lawyer's office to sign them. So technically he was still married when he died. Mother was always sorry that I wasn't ever going to get married. She finally had to accept that, too, along with everything else. I know she's going to adore you."

By the time the plane touched down in Atlanta, I was picturing the meeting with Charles's family as a scene from *Suddenly, Last Summer.*

Charles's nieces and nephews were milling around the lawn in front of their suburban Atlanta home, waiting to be introduced. They had odd names, Sprice, Linna, Levi . . . I couldn't keep track of them all. I sensed Charles's concern that everything run smoothly, that I be comfortable with his family, so I made an effort to engage each nephew and niece in conversation. I found it easiest to talk with Bessie, the oldest daughter, a beautiful teenager graduating that year from high school. She was considering becoming an opera singer herself and was excited about seeing Martile. She had just played the role of Peter Pan in her school musical, and she showed me selections from a videotape of the performance. Fortunately, she was exceptionally talented, so I was able to be genuinely complimentary.

While we were watching the tape, Charles's mother arrived, having driven from Augusta. I went to meet her on the front lawn. She was a slender, white-haired woman with an engaging smile, in her seventies, soft-spoken with a strong Georgia accent. There were hugs for all her grandchildren. Then everybody went about their tasks in the house, and in a matter of minutes I found myself alone with Evelyn on the back deck, where a redheaded woodpecker was perched at a feeder.

Her first words to me were, "Well, I suppose Charles has told you all about our dysfunctional family."

I liked her right away.

Despite my concerns about how a Mormon family might treat two visiting gay men, it never seemed to be an issue. They gave us the boys' bedroom, where there were two very narrow single beds. Partly out of respect, but more for comfort, we slept in separate beds.

The next night when Charles and I were at a restaurant having dinner before the opera, our waiter continually kept forgetting to bring me my silverware. Our entrées sat on plates in front of us, time was passing, the performance was to begin soon. Charles had his silverware but refused to begin eating until I could. He reminded the waiter twice, without results. I could see Charles getting more and more irritated. Finally, he got up, disappeared into the kitchen, which startled me, and returned with a knife and fork. No one had ever done such a thing for me. I was giddy with delight.

The waiter rushed out of the kitchen, alarmed.

"Don't mind me," Charles said without glancing at him. "I work at a restaurant. You should bring the silverware to the table before the customer is served."

I was getting the picture that Charles did not tolerate sloppiness, in any situation, and had no qualms about letting someone know that he disapproved. I decided I must never do anything sloppily again.

It had been important to me for Charles to see and hear Martile in person, after all my talk about her. I was a little nervous, because anything can go wrong in an operatic performance. When we walked into the old Fox Theater, where the opera season was held in Atlanta, I knew right away we were in for something special. The interior of the theater was an old-fashioned Hollywood mishmash of ancient Egyptian, Moorish, and Babylonian architecture, crammed with columns, desert-sheik tents, and palm trees, like a Cecil B. De-Mille epic, with a dark blue, star-studded plaster ceiling over the entire audience, the perfect setting for Verdi's over-the-top Victorian melodrama of counts, Gypsies, and the wrong baby thrown into the flames.

Charles and Martile finally got to meet, backstage after the first performance, after each being so curious about the other. Martile was formidable in full operatic stage makeup, but six-foot-four Charles towered over her. The two larger-than-life, self-exiled Southerners took to each other instantly. It sounded to me as if their long-submerged southern accents had bubbled up to the surface for the occasion. I was happy that these two people, each so important in my life, were getting along so well.

"How did I do?" Martile asked me. She knew I would always be honest with her.

"Martile, that was the most fabulous Leonora since the days of Zinka Milanov!"

"Well, I can't do better than that, can I?" she said.

The next morning, Charles and I had breakfast with Martile at an IHOP. Martile was a little bleary after the opening-night excitement, but she had pulled herself together in diva fashion, her bright red hair teased out to twice its volume. The waitresses poured on thick southern hospitality, calling us "Shugah" and "Dahhlin'." As soon as they were out of earshot, Martile said, "You know, the South is the only place where they've elevated terms of endearment to the highest form of hypocrisy. Don't you just know they're back there in the kitchen saying, 'Did y'all see her hair!' "

I had been concerned about the Atlanta trip, our first trip together, because so often traveling with a new lover can bring out disastrous incompatibilities; but it was all comfortable and remarkably easy, as if we'd been traveling together for years.

Charles's two sisters had not come to Atlanta, but they did come to celebrate Evelyn's seventy-fifth birthday in Orient. Frieda flew in from Chicago, and Angel drove down from her new home in Providence, Rhode Island, via the Orient Point–

New London ferry. That was the first time I met either of them, after hearing so much about them. It was also the first time the three siblings and their mother had been together in a couple of years. I sensed Charles was apprehensive about the visit. I knew it was important to him that I liked his family.

Frieda and Angel were each almost as tall as Charles, and each had an imposing presence. It quickly became apparent that they had issues, with each other and with their mother. I didn't know the backstories. Charles kept his patience and was carefully considerate to all three of them, but I could see the tension mounting in him.

I suggested a short drive to show off Orient, first the historic houses along Village Lane and then the state park, where I knew the road would be bordered by rugosa roses as it stretched into the glittering bay. While Charles drove, acting as tour guide, the conversation between Evelyn and her daughters got sandpapery. One issue had to do with making Evelyn's famous strawberry shortcake for her birthday. Frieda was adamant about using only aluminum-free baking powder, which I was not sure we could find locally. Evelyn said it didn't matter if we used regular baking powder. Frieda and Angel argued about it. Charles was losing his patience; I was getting nervous. Back in our driveway, Frieda and Angel stormed out of the car in different directions, with Charles following first one and then the other. I was left alone with Charles's mother once again, just as we had been on that back porch in Atlanta.

She turned to me and said, in her soft drawl, "My two boys turned out just fine, but I sure don't know what went wrong with my girls."

I thought about the first time my own mother had come to visit, in 1983, soon after I bought the house. It was a bright, sunny day then, too, but there was no garden yet, no roses, just the old house standing in an empty field behind its low privet hedge, and four neon pink azaleas that tinged the white shingles with their reflection. My aunts Pennie and Edna came along with my mother, who had just turned eighty. The beginning signs of her senility were still two years away. Pennie, the eldest and already out of it, was cheerful and giggly, about what no one had any idea. Edna was a few years younger and had not yet been diagnosed with the colon cancer that would kill her. My aunt Valerie, the youngest of the sisters, had come up from Boca Raton to join them, nut-brown from golfing in the Florida sun. I have a photograph of the four women in front of the house, standing just behind the privet hedge against a backdrop of garish azaleas at peak bloom. My mother and my aunts, each one clutching a big fake-leather handbag, are smiling for the camera but they do not look comfortable. That is because they did not understand this house or why I wanted it. I knew what they were thinking while I was taking the picture, and it saddened me then as it does now when I look at the watercolor I painted from it.

They could not, could never, understand the old wooden floors that sagged with age, the peeling paint that showed three hundred years of different colors and hinted at three hundred years' worth of lives lived in the house. They wandered from room to room, clucking their tongues, my mother nudging Edna with her elbow and pointing out some defect, a broken windowpane or a loose doorjamb, rolling her eyes significantly in the family manner. They could not imagine the garden I yearned to make in the flat field behind the house.

My mother had never understood why I was so happy in Orient. There was no way for me to explain if she could not see it with her own eyes and feel it in her own heart. When

They did not understand this house or why I wanted it.

we visited Freddie's home on Orchard Street, at the edge of farmland, its field of Queen Anne's lace stretching out from the porch toward the wetlands, the bay sparkling in the distance, the sky full of Constable clouds, Freddie exclaimed, "Isn't this a ravishing view?"

"What view?" my mother asked in all seriousness. "What's there to look at?"

But Charles's mother and sisters were interested in everything about Orient. They saw the beauty in it all, even in our slightly dilapidated home. Frieda wandered the garden with her camera, saying she could use the photographs in her artwork. Angel became inspired by the idea of gardening at her new home in Providence. Evelyn loved the roses and the birds. At first, Charles's family had seemed exotic to me, and the tense dynamics between the two sisters and between mother and daughters unnerved me. I was relieved to see that they welcomed me as Charles's partner.

My mother and her sisters had never been welcoming to outsiders. They didn't trust anyone who was not, as they termed it, "a member of the family."

As a child, I used to spend weekends with my maiden aunts Tessie and Pennie in their Washington Heights two-bedroom apartment, which they shared with my grandmother and an unmarried uncle, Allie, who worked nights at a saloon and slept all day. Tessie and Pennie slept in a bedroom with my grandmother, Tessie in her own narrow bed, Pennie next to her mother in a double bed. Uncle Allie's bedroom was on the other side of the bathroom. They lived this closely all their lives, only gaining a little privacy as one after another of them died, Allie first from cancer.

As a child, I saw nothing odd about this arrangement. I figured that spending an entire life with your family, never having privacy, never having a special friend, even sleeping all your life in your mother's bed, was something that happened to people sometimes. I hoped it wouldn't happen to me, but it was a worrisome possibility.

During the daytime it was a household of women. My grandmother Ida, broad and squat, sat silent all day in a red leather wing chair in the dark "sunken" living room, listening to radio soap operas. She looked like George Washington as he is carved onto Mount Rushmore. The story I was told was that she had never again left the house after an incident in a department store when her umbrella jammed the escalator and everyone fell down like dominoes. Now she sat in her wing chair, afraid of the outside world.

Aunt Tessie, the eldest, was tall and big-boned like her sisters, but unlike them she was rail thin, her exaggerated cheekbones and long nose giving her the look of Marlene Dietrich reflected in a fun-house mirror. She had never worked outside the house, but at home she was an avid seamstress, sitting for hours by the bedroom window sewing elaborate outfits for herself and her sisters, chain-smoking Camels, and occasionally burning holes in the fabric. She would camouflage these cigarette holes with intricate ruchings, pleatings, and appliqués, whether or not the pattern called for them. I loved watching her sew, loved all her sewing paraphernalia, loved the crunch of her pinking scissors cutting around patterns, the crinkling sound of the tissue paper, the pins she held in her tightly pressed lips clicking against her false teeth, the snap of thread after she'd stitched a knot. Tessie's extravagant hand-sewn ensembles, with matching gloves, hats, and bags, earned her the family nickname Stella Dallas, the title character on one of my grandmother's radio soap operas, a "clothes horse," as was said in the 1950s. Tessie rarely had any place to go dressed up like that except to family funerals.

Pennie worked in a button factory, hand-painting decorations on buttons and buckles. Her real name was Olga, but she had swallowed a penny as a child and the nickname stuck. She was plain and dumpy, had whiskers on her chin, and was clumsy, often falling in the street for no apparent reason. Pennie taught me to paint the stylized flamingos and palm trees she produced at work, popular decorative motifs in the fifties. I could knock out a palm tree one-two-three, criss-crosses all up the trunk and a flourish of leaves at the top, a few coconuts dabbed in, a Pepto-Bismol pink flamingo on either side.

Friday evenings I'd watch out the window with my aunts, waiting for another aunt, Edna, to walk past on her way home from the subway station. Edna lived alone in a small apartment further along Fort Washington Avenue. She would knock on my aunts' ground-floor windows as she passed and then come around through the building entrance to have dinner with us. Edna worked as a secretary in the New York office of Twentieth Century-Fox. She often brought me publicity stills of popular movie stars, young Marilyn Monroe and upstart flashes in the pan like Sheree North, Jayne Mansfield, and Terry Moore that Fox was promoting. Every now and then she would get us all tickets to premières (a foreign-sounding word that I was thrilled to learn and to pronounce) at the Roxy, an ornately decorated, old-fashioned movie palace.

One evening Edna brought me eight-by-ten glossies of Elvis Presley. I must have been about eleven, because his first film, *Love Me Tender,* was in 1956. I knew all the words to the title song, but I didn't sound anything like Elvis when I sang it. Nor did I look anything like him, with my pale blond hair, even though I tried to copy his clothes. I knew some people thought he was bad.

"I don't see what all the controversy is about," Edna said at dinner, referring to Elvis's appearance on *The Ed Sullivan*

Show, where he had been shown only from the waist up, since there was much talk about his gyrating hips. I didn't dare tell anyone I had a crush on Elvis Presley. I didn't even understand it myself. I only knew I felt cheated by not getting to see him from the waist down. "Heartbreak Hotel," his big hit, said it all for me. I played that 45 over and over.

My aunts' bedroom looked onto Fort Washington Avenue just above the building's entrance, where the rose of Sharons stretched long branches in search of sun. Tessie and Pennie passed hours at the window commenting on familiar passersby, for whom my aunts had particular nicknames even though they did not know these people at all.

"Look, here comes Blondie," Pennie would say about a skinny woman with bleached hair piled elaborately atop her head in Marie Antoinette fashion. She'd cluck her tongue at Blondie's outfit. "Such finery!"

"And here come the Widlischers," Tessie would point out, sucking on a Camel and exhaling strong smoke, referring to a peculiar couple, an old woman and a young man, maybe mother and son, but who knew for sure? The two odd strangers wore heavy winter coats all year and had cotton stuffed into their ears. They looked like they never washed. I'd watch them disappear up Fort Washington Avenue to who knew where. They made me feel sad. Maybe I saw in them a scary future for myself and my mother.

My aunts seemed happier to watch the world go past than to be a part of it. But for me, that street, running out of sight north and south, represented the whole outside world for which I longed but into which I was too young to be let loose. To the north were Fort Tryon Park's tiered gardens and the Cloisters. To the south lay "downtown" with its Broadway musicals, the Roxy, Radio City, Ruby Foo's Chinese restaurant, and streets teeming with dangerous, intriguing people.

I'd seen these places only with my mother's hand holding mine tight. I couldn't imagine how I was ever going to get out into them on my own.

Once I did get out into the world on my own, I took advantage of every opportunity to travel as far from home as possible, through the Mediterranean countries, both in Europe and North Africa, to South America, to Asia. Of course I wanted to see the famous sites and taste the exotic foods, but really I was always looking for romance. I never found it on those trips. When I had a home of my own in Orient, I was less interested in traveling. And now that Charles and I were creating a garden there together, I wanted to stay at home.

I was comforted that Charles's mother and sisters appreciated how much we loved Orient. They were interested in everything from the multicolored pebbles on the beach to the ospreys on their huge, elaborate nests atop structures that had been erected to entice the majestic birds to settle. My own mother and aunts had paid no attention to such local sights. I had already learned from Charles that his mother was so devoted to wildlife that each year she volunteered to help baby turtles make it down the beach to the sea, that she had turned her own lot into a wildlife sanctuary.

"It's just a suburban corner lot in Augusta," Evelyn said.

Charles was quick to add, "All her neighbors have lawns and typical shrubs, but Mother has planted shrubs that produce fruits and berries for the birds. She's got a huge Cherokee rose, that's the Georgia state flower. It grows out of control. And enormous pyracanthas. The birds love their berries. Those bushes have horrible thorns, and they grow fast down there. Whenever I visit, I prune them for her, just to keep them away from the house. And she hangs hummingbird feeders all over the property. Skip, tell Mother your hummingbird story!"

Charles knew I liked to tell this story. I recounted to Evelyn how one summer day, soon after I had bought the house, I was watering the garden when a male ruby-throated hummingbird flew right up to the nozzle of the hose to drink from it, its wings whirring, suspended an inch from my fingers. It was so astonishing, so magical, that time slowed for me. He couldn't have been there for more than a few seconds, splashing around in the spray, close enough to touch, but I didn't want the moment to end and so it seemed it never would.

Friends asked to see him, too. I'd get out the hose, and sure enough, the hummingbird came back again and again. All that summer, he never disappointed anyone who came to see him. I nicknamed him Dinger, short for Humdinger. Each time I went out into the garden, I would see him fly overhead and alight on the tallest branch of the weeping Alaska cedar, like a bright Christmas angel on the very top. I'd call out, "Hello, Dinger! Come have your bath!" He'd wait up there, watching, until I turned on the water. Then he'd buzz down, perch on a shrub nearby, and let me spray him while he flapped his wings and ruffled his iridescent feathers and sipped droplets of water. Dinger visited only that one summer, and never again.

"Was your mother always a gardener?" I asked Charles when we had some time to ourselves. I was trying to distract him, to get him to relax about the family visit, which so far had kept him tense and on the lookout for trouble.

"Mother didn't have time to garden when she was raising us. She always got up early and cooked a big southern breakfast for all of us. Grits and eggs and homemade biscuits. She made the biscuits from scratch every morning. And every night she had dinner ready. She was trained as a nurse and knew all about nutrition, so dinner was always carefully balanced. After school she drove each of us to music lessons or other appointments. She did the laundry and housecleaning. The garden was something that was just there, around the house. A yard."

"Did you have a part of the garden that was your own?"

"I had my own dogwood tree. Once my mother brought back four little dogwood trees, one for each of us. They were no more than sticks, really. I don't know where she got them. We were each supposed to take care of our own tree. Which was just watering them, basically."

"Did they all live?"

"I took care of mine, so mine did. I don't remember what happened to Frieda's. Bill was still a little kid and Angel couldn't have been more than an infant, so my mother must have taken care of those. And we had a few roses planted around the yard. I guess they were hybrid teas, just typical ones you could get in those days. They never did well. The summers are too hot and humid down there. They were always scraggly, sickly things. But every summer Mother would take us to a nursery and we'd bring back new roses to plant."

We had plenty of roses to show Evelyn that June, all our treasured old-fashioned varieties. Ivory-petaled 'Madame Alfred Carriere' was clambering into the 'New Dawn' in front of which I photographed Charles hugging his mother, and nearby a huge bush of *Rosa moschata plena*, with flowers like apple blossoms, perfumed the garden for yards around. 'Rosarie de l'Hay', a hybrid rugosa with big magenta flowers swirled with crumpled petals, was in full bloom. Nearby was another hybrid rugosa, 'Rose à Parfum de l'Hay', this one a deep opera-velvet red. Both names are nods to the famous French rose garden at Hay, and each of the roses has its own intense perfume. Then there was my favorite, the mid-nineteenth-century old-rose pink 'Madame Isaac Pereire', the most fragrant of all, and Charles's favorite, Griffith Buck's pristine white 'Paloma Blanca'. And the rose we'd planted especially for his mother, David Austin's 'Evelyn'.

"The visit is going well," I ventured to Charles, aware that he was exhausted.

"I love them," he said, wearily, "but when all three of them get together, it's really difficult."

Charles's sisters both came back to Orient to see his exhibition at the Oysterponds Historical Society, but it was too long a trip for Evelyn to make again from Augusta. Charles was in overdrive with the excitement of showing them his collection, so having the three Dean siblings all together at once in our little Village Lane home was daunting for me. I wondered what I had gotten myself into. But there was always the garden for refuge. I could opt out of participating by saying there was weeding to be done.

The garden attracted as many visitors as did the exhibition. Charles was less comfortable with people arriving unannounced at all hours than I was. Whenever I ran into friends who said, "Let's get together," I'd say, "Come see the garden," rather than make a date, which might get in the way of something I'd rather do. Everyone took me up on the offer.

"It's like Grand Central Station," Charles said when one group of visitors arrived just as another left.

Once I overheard him on the phone saying, in his best Carlyle Restaurant manner, "So it will be a party of two?"

"What was that about?" I asked.

"I don't know who it was. Two friends of yours said they're coming to see the garden."

Our friend Karen, three houses down Village Lane, came to visit daily—often several times a day—to see the garden in different lights. She liked to joke that when she first met me, I said I worked at a nursery, and when she first met Charles, he told her he was a waiter. There had been no mention of Charles's print collection or of my past career as a set designer and trompe l'oeil painter, or of my writing.

Karen and I had met when I was selling small watercolors of local landscapes at Eighteenth-Century Day, an annual fund-raiser for the historical society. After explaining that she was just looking, that she couldn't buy artwork because she was still buying necessities—silverware, furniture, rugs, and so on for the house she had just moved into—she returned to my table and bought a watercolor of the boulders at Youngs Road Beach, an iconic portrait of our favorite swimming spot. We got to know each other over that summer whenever she dropped by the garden for advice. Karen and her husband, Mike, and their two sons had moved into their house about the time Charles and I met, and now she was interested in learning about gardening. One day, when I mentioned to her that I was a writer but had never had anything published, she said, "You know Mike and I have a publishing house, don't you?" I told her no, I did not.

Soon after that, she visited the garden while I was deep into weeding and announced, "I have a proposal to make. I want to publish an anthology of poems and stories for gardeners, and I want you and Charles to edit it."

I was flabbergasted. "Neither of us has ever edited anything."

"It doesn't matter. Look at this garden! And you both love to read. You two are the right people to edit this book."

Charles and I talked it over, and we decided to plunge in. We worked for two years, spending long hours at the public library at Forty-second Street, photocopying and reading several hundred short stories and poems, everything from Hawaiian folktales to translations of German short stories. I gathered the stories, while Charles gathered the poems, because he was a more experienced reader of poetry. We amassed cardboard boxes and plastic grocery bags full of photocopies, without order or unifying theme. Karen guided us through the whole process. We never doubted her judgment, and tiring as the work was, we enjoyed every minute of it.

One day, Karen announced, "Okay, now we have to start figuring out what this book is about. You probably won't know until the night before it's done."

We began to narrow our selections. All of a sudden it became apparent that what we wanted was to capture the essence of what it is *to be a gardener.*

No pretty poems about lovely trees or stories about delightful strolls in the woods or tales of Hawaiian spirits. We wanted works that explained why anyone would get down on his or her knees in the mud while it was cold and raining to care for a plant. We edited the hundreds of works down to twelve poems and twelve stories.

"That's it!" Karen exclaimed. "And I want the book to have illustrations."

"But each of these stories and poems is in a different style. I don't see how this book can be illustrated."

"You'll come up with something," Karen said. "They'll have to be black-and-white. Anyway, I'm not worried."

I *was* worried, but after fiddling around with many unsuccessful approaches, it occurred to Charles and me that what was needed was not an illustration for each story and poem but a series of illustrations that stood on their own. Twelve illustrations, twelve stories, twelve poems: That would be the book. We chose portraits of twelve of our favorite plants from Charles's garden photographs, and I painted the illustrations based on them, using Japanese *sumi* ink to get subtle gradations of black in an attempt to capture the essence of the plants without using color.

When Karen asked us to write the introduction, Charles and I decided to do this separately and then compare and combine our efforts. One evening, he called from the city to read his version to me over the phone. "I begin mine with: 'We garden,'" he said.

"So do I!" I read him my beginning sentence.

"I bet we wrote the same introduction!"

We read each other our own versions and discovered that they were pretty much identical in content.

"I think this is a good sign," I said. "Maybe it means we know what we are doing after all."

The result was *Of Leaf and Flower.* Included were short stories by writers as diverse as John Updike and Eugenia Collier, and poems by Cynthia Zarin and Mark Doty, among others. We held a book signing at the nursery where I worked and sold over three hundred books that afternoon, which Karen thought was remarkable. We expected close friends to each buy a book, to be supportive. But what was amazing and encouraging was that so many people who bought one book came back later in the day, after they'd had a chance to look at it, to buy several more to give as gifts.

We were invited to give a reading of selections from the anthology at the historical society. It would be an outdoor event, with chairs and a lectern set up on the greensward in front of the schoolhouse. Charles and I were nervous that morning, neither of us being experienced readers. As we were getting ready to walk down Village Lane, Charles called out from the back porch, "Honeybun, come look at this!"

He was holding a pot of butterfly amaryllis, which he had grown for years in the city apartment. It never bloomed there, and he had said he was going to put it down the incinerator chute, but I had urged him to spare it and bring it out to Orient for the summer. Now, as he presented it to me, I saw

that it was in full bloom. Big maroon flowers veined in chartreuse capped each stalk. Just in time for the reading! We
carried it down to the schoolhouse and set it on the lectern.

"Anything can happen in a garden," Charles began, and
told the story of the amaryllis's unexpected first bloom.

The Garden Writers Association awarded my illustrations for *Of Leaf and Flower* their Garden Globe for Best Book
Illustration that year. Usually this award went to technical
botanical illustrations. I was surprised that they had chosen
my romanticized plant portraits. Charles and I flew out to
Seattle for the award ceremony. While we were there, we visited Heronswood Nursery on Bainbridge Island, finally seeing in person the facility from which we had ordered so many
of the unusual plants that were treasures in our garden.

One morning later that summer, while Charles was in the
city, the World Trade Center towers were struck by planes
and collapsed. Once I learned about it, I went to a friend's
house to see the news on television, since we did not have one
in our home. I couldn't bear to watch. I went back to our
garden, where it was a warm blue-sky day. A hummingbird
was working the salvias, suspended awhile at each flower's
throat before moving on to tend another, its slender beak disappearing into each floret and sliding out again with the
carefulness of an expert botanist intent on hybridizing. Monarchs were on the buddleias, lazily cavorting, silent copper on
violet. And there were bees.

If I could have flown high above the garden, higher and
higher, I might have seen the green crab claw of Long Island
finely outlined by its pale sand beaches, crisp and clear to
where it joined Manhattan, only to disappear into poisonous
smoke.

I was frantic. I couldn't reach Charles. The telephone lines were busy, or dead. We were supposed to go up to Ithaca that weekend to attend a lecture given by Dan Hinkley, the founder of Heronswood Nursery. But I learned from the news reports that no one was allowed in or out of Manhattan. Bridges and tunnels were shut. Television showed flashing road signs reading MANHATTAN CLOSED, the most disturbing notice I had ever seen. Edwin was in the air on his way back from visiting his new friend, Tim, in South Africa. He was grounded in England for ten days. Charles would not be able to get out to Orient for ten days. Although our neighborhood on the Upper East Side was not endangered, I could only picture him in a fog of poisoned air while the garden went on blossoming with late-summer flowers, humming with the determined business of bees. I wanted him with me, safe in our garden.

There was personal tragedy that year as well. Evelyn, now eighty, had been diagnosed with ALS. Having been a nurse all her life, she knew exactly what to expect from the disease: that she would slowly lose control of her muscles, become increasingly paralyzed, and finally be unable to swallow. She planned to die at home, on her own terms. She had mapped it all out and organized everything, even her own funeral. After the World Trade Center attack, Frieda, whose Manhattan apartment was near Ground Zero and had become uninhabitable, went down to live with her mother in Augusta, to care for her, so that Evelyn could remain in her own home. Charles and I visited early on, while Evelyn was still able to move her arms and legs.

She had a funny little long-haired, black-and-white dog at that time, Snowball, that had been rescued, starving and ill, from along a Georgia highway. Evelyn's nursing skills had brought the dog back to full health. Snowball was the size of a small terrier, with a foxy muzzle, floppy ears, tousled black hair, and white paws. She loved visitors, but she was very polite. Even though she clearly wanted to greet me, she would flatten herself on the floor at my feet, like a miniature bear rug, her nose by my toes, her eyes looking up imploringly, waiting to be invited onto my lap. "Okay!" I'd say, and then she would leap up happily and lick my face. I fell in love with her.

"She's the sweetest dog I ever saw," I told Charles. "If we ever get a dog, I want one just like Snowball."

"She's a mutt. We'll never find one exactly like her."

While we were visiting, we drove up to Knoxville, where Charles had grown up. The Knoxville Museum of Art was hosting an exhibition of Charles's collection, now comprising almost twice as many prints as had been shown in Orient. The setting in the more formal and professional institution added new luster to the collection. Charles's only regret was that his mother was not well enough to make the trip.

To give Frieda a break, Charles flew down to see Evelyn whenever he could get off from work. When he was here with me up north, the phone conversations with his mother devastated him. Frieda would hold the phone for Evelyn as she inexorably deteriorated.

One October day, while Charles and I were sitting in the Orient living room, Frieda called. As I watched Charles talk, I saw tears run down his cheeks, but he was smiling when he repeated Frieda's words to me.

"The most amazing thing has happened," he explained. "All the trees and shrubs on Mother's property are filled with hummingbirds, hundreds of them. All along every branch of every tree."

"They must have stopped on their migration south," I said.

"Frieda has wheeled Mother's bed close to the window,"

Charles related. "Mother said she's never seen anything like it, in all the years she's been there."

Charles was sobbing, his whole body trembling. I wanted to comfort him, but I didn't want to interfere in this private moment. He told Frieda to hold the phone to his mother's ear. He was trying to control his voice. Through his tears, he managed to say, "Mother, they know how much you have always loved them. They've come to say good-bye."

Evelyn died that November.

Frances and Victor

Soon after I bought my house, a longtime resident taught me an Orient tradition of wishing on a full moon observed through a Holey Stone, which is a beach pebble with a hole worn all the way through by erosion or perhaps by a tiny determined sea creature.

"You must line the hole up with the full moon showing through its center," she explained. "Only then may the wish be made."

These stones are not easy to find. You have to spend a lot of time sifting through beach pebbles and holding each one up to try to see blue sky through the hole. You discard a lot before you come across one with a hole all the way through. I have bowls of Holey Stones in the house—gray, pink, yellow, orange, maroon, black, or striped or dotted in a combination of colors—each stone brought back from a walk on the beach.

For years, on the night of a full moon, I would select a stone from one of the bowls, carry it out through the back porch, and hold it up to the sky to center the moon through it. The wish I always made was for someone with whom I could share my garden.

Then I met Charles, who is not the least superstitious or

inclined to such malarkey. But when I heard that the last full moon of the millennium, which was to fall on the winter solstice, was predicted to be the closest and brightest in our lifetime, I thought that maybe wishes made on that unique full moon would be more readily fulfilled. I urged Charles to select a Holey Stone from one of the bowls. I picked one that looked powerful, and we drove to the nearby wetlands beach to watch the moon rise. That December evening sky was clear, the air unusually mild for winter and remarkably still, but a chilly breeze came up as we stood on the damp sand facing an open view over the water. The calm bay reflected the sky, darkening in the east but turquoise and orange in the west. A great blue heron took flight in silhouette against the glow.

Across the bay, behind a line of bare trees, the full moon climbed quickly, pumpkin-colored and lopsided, spilling its tremulous orange reflection toward us onto the mirrored surface of the water.

We each looked at the moon through our own Holey Stone. Each of us made our private wish.

Charles and I had been together for four years. I wished for many more.

Working as a landscaper, I got poison ivy every summer, at least once and sometimes repeatedly, no matter how careful I was. I treated it myself, with drying ointments and gauze bandages. I've always had a phobia about going to doctors, so I would ignore the blisters and will the rash to get well, and eventually it did. The first summer Charles and I were together, I got an especially bad rash with unusually large open blisters. I wrapped my wrists so thickly with gauze that it looked to some people like I had slit them in a suicide attempt. Charles was startled to learn that I wasn't planning to see a doctor. One night at dinner in Greenport, Charles's expression across the table actually scared me as he watched me fork spaghetti with one hand and arm completely swathed in ooze-stained gauze.

"I don't know," he said coldly. "Maybe you are someone whose judgment I cannot trust."

His words and tone sent a cold tremor through me. I saw my doctor the next day and got a cortisone injection. Charles was pleased. The rash healed quickly.

When Charles turned fifty in 1999, he pointed out that neither one of us had had a colonoscopy and scheduled his appointment. Maybe because his mother had been a nurse, he was not frightened by medical things the way I was. On the walk down Madison Avenue from our apartment to his doctor's office, our fears unspoken that the procedure might result in finding cancer, we discussed instead which of us would be willing to outlive the other. It seemed kinder to let the one you love die first, to spare him the pain of grief and loneliness. "You can die first." "No, you can!" We each promised we were willing to be the sorrowful survivor. I wished it would never happen, either way.

I sat in Dr. Katzman's waiting room while Charles had the procedure. I had brought a notebook, intending to write, to keep my mind from wandering to all the possible dire outcomes, but I couldn't concentrate. The notebook lay open on my lap. Instead, I let myself be mesmerized by a not-very-good oil painting on the wall. It showed the interior of a glass greenhouse, a woman in a shapeless blue dress carrying a tray of seedlings. I pretended this woman was a modern Joséphine Bonaparte in her own contemporary Malmaison greenhouse, because I had been reading about Joséphine recently and was fascinated by her passion for hybridizing roses. The

odd, bulbous seedlings in the painting could have been anything. Figuring out what they might be was a good way to
take my mind off Charles. I decided they were jade plants.
What other plants are in this painting? I wondered. A philodendron, a dracaena, maybe an agave. Hard to tell—the
painting was so bad. On the bench behind the woman: red
salvias and lilac geraniums, perhaps. The colors were awful.
This diverted my attention for a few seconds, but not long
enough.

I had told Charles that if he got anxious during the procedure he should picture himself walking down our garden
paths and visualize what was in bloom now, what would be in
bloom in a month, in two months. That's how I had always
gotten myself through doctors' appointments. Now, as I sat
waiting, I pictured where I'd plant the zinnia seedlings and
the summer-flowering bulbs. I imagined where I'd move the
volunteer cleome and *Verbena bonariensis* seedlings that were
already everywhere they shouldn't be in the garden. I would
leave some wherever they had sprung up. I always do, because there is no way to predict what picture they will create.
Charles would rip them out, of course, but I replanted and
replaced and replanted again, waiting for Charles to come
out of the procedure room.

I was glad when one of the nurses struck up a conversation. Her voice had a charming Hispanic lilt.

"What are you writing?" she asked, indicating the open
notebook on my knees, and when I told her it was a garden
memoir she said, "I have a terrace garden, and it is so important to me. I take care of my plants each morning before I
come to work and each evening when I get home. Now I am
teaching my ten-year-old son to care for his own plant just as
he would care for his own body."

I was touched by her story, and briefly distracted.

Charles had been gone for two hours by then. I had understood these procedures generally last about forty-five minutes. I heard a groan from down the hall. Why did he just groan? Was it pain, or had he heard bad news? The nurse seemed unconcerned, busy at her desk. I pictured again where I'd plant my zinnias. Here; no, there; no, over there. Why was this taking so long?

Charles still did not come out of the procedure room.

I started thinking about which tree we ought to plant on our grave site. Charles had recently bought two adjoining plots in Orient's Central Cemetery, in what he called the "gay section," because so many of our friends had selected plots in that area. But we planned not to be buried there. We both wanted to be cremated and for our ashes to be cast somewhere yet to be decided. I thought perhaps in our garden, but then, what if the next owner bulldozed everything and started over with a lawn? That wasn't appealing. Maybe I'd want my ashes scattered in the Sound. But where might the currents carry them? To Connecticut? I didn't want to spend eternity in New London.

Anyway, we would not be buried in the Orient cemetery. Instead, we had the idea to plant one tree on our two plots, with a bronze plaque or carved stone marker reading: THIS TREE WAS PLANTED BY CHARLES DEAN AND CLYDE WACHS-BERGER, and the date. It would grow huge. For generations our names would be connected with that magnificent tree. We had considered certain trees and changed our minds again and again. Should it be evergreen? Then maybe a deodar cedar—particularly the powder blue variety 'Karl Fuchs', one of which had died in our own garden. Or should it be a flowering tree? A pink-flowered yellowwood, since we had a white-flowered one in our garden. Or a southern magnolia, both evergreen and flowering. But the deer would destroy that. Deer resistance was a consideration. Other considerations were size (not so big as to overhang neighboring graves) and hardiness. But above all it should be a tree with serene presence.

I looked across to the nurse, still doing paperwork. I did not want to interrupt her again to ask why it was taking so long.

The previous day on National Public Radio I had heard a snippet of a piece about the ancient Greek myth of Baucis and Philemon. This old, happily married wife and husband were devoted to each other, and their hospitality to strangers (sometimes clever gods in disguise) was so admired that they were granted their fondest wish—that they never be separated from each other. As a reward, the kindly gods turned them into two trees growing side by side with their branches intertwined. Sitting in Dr. Katzman's office, I got the idea to plant two trees on the grave site, trees that would grow forever next to each other. Some stately tree for Charles and a shorter one for me, companion trees.

I reminded myself always to be hospitable to strangers.

"Here he comes now," the nurse said.

Charles walked into the waiting room, wobbly from the anesthesia. It scared me to see him unsteady on his feet, Charles, so tall, who always seemed so in charge. I feigned calmness and helped him into the hard plastic seat next to me. He was pale and trembling and almost missed the chair.

"The doctor says I don't have cancer, Honeybun," he managed to whisper in a groggy voice as I held a Styrofoam glass of ginger ale for him.

For the moment I stopped thinking about our grave site trees and switched to the trees we wanted for our garden.

.

In May 2005, Charles and I brought back two rare 'Silver Parasol' magnolias, grown for us from cuttings at the Arnold Arboretum in Boston. We'd been waiting five years for these trees.

The adventure had started in 2000 with my meeting Frances Leventritt, an elderly, eccentric, wealthy widow living at the Carlyle. Charles had known her for years because she regularly dined in the restaurant, always at table 26, known as "Mrs. Leventritt's table." When Charles called me late at night from the city after he got home from work, he usually had stories about the outrageous thing she'd said or done that night.

"She was a great beauty in her youth," he told me. "I think she was a Ziegfeld Follies girl, or something like that, but you'd never know it now. She always comes down to the restaurant in an old housecoat, and she's very particular and demanding, and she has no qualms about using profanities, and I mean really loudly, when she isn't satisfied with something. Sometimes when other customers call for a reservation, they ask me, 'Is *she* here tonight?' and if I say yes, they decide to eat somewhere else."

One day Charles called to say, "Mrs. Leventritt wants to meet you!"

"Why?" I was slightly horrified.

"Because I've told her all about you. She loves opera. I told her you were a big fan of Zinka Milanov, and it turns out she was, too. And she loves plants and gardens. I've shown her pictures of our garden. I've arranged for you to have high tea with her next Tuesday. Be prepared for anything from genteel kindness to gutter rudeness."

That Tuesday, Mrs. Leventritt kept me waiting more than an hour before she made her mind up to come downstairs to the Carlyle dining room. Even though Charles had prepared me, when she finally entered the elegant room I was startled. In came an old woman bent over a walker, seemingly in great pain from crippling arthritis, wearing a shabby housecoat and shuffling along in loose slippers, her gray hair in a disheveled bun.

"Who put this crap on my table?" she demanded, lowering her bulk awkwardly into a sitting position on the banquette, careless of how her housecoat flopped open over her slip and flour-white knees. "You know I don't want this crap on my table." She pushed away the graceful knife and fork at her place setting. "Get it off here!"

Charles replaced them with a smaller salad fork and knife, which seemed to mollify her.

I had been told she was in her eighties, but she still had a pink baby face, mischievous piercing blue eyes, and—when she wanted to turn it on—a coy schoolgirlish manner. She made me nervous, but we hit it off because of our shared love of opera. In fact, Mrs. Leventritt had briefly tried a career as an operatic soprano herself. That hadn't worked out, she told me, because of some sort of throat disorder.

"But I never had a problem telling conductors exactly where to put their batons," she bragged.

She did get a part in a revival of *Showboat*.

I knew from Charles that as a showgirl she had attracted the eye of a prominent lawyer named M. Victor Leventritt, a Harvard graduate, married him, and was now an incredibly wealthy widow. That did not stop her from refusing to pay the check when Charles delivered it to our table.

"He's *your* friend," she snapped at Charles. "You set this up. Why should I pay for it?"

Charles picked up the tab graciously, as if it were only proper.

At that time, Dr. Robert Cook, the director of the Arnold

Arboretum, was wooing Mrs. Leventritt for a three-million-dollar gift to fund a new vine and shrub garden, which would be named after her and her late husband. She had already given millions over the years to Harvard, and to the arboretum, to honor her husband, and she was likely to continue because she loved plants and wildlife with a passion. But her arthritis prevented her from traveling to Boston, so one night at the Carlyle, in front of Dr. Cook, she told Charles she wanted him to take me to have a look at the piece of land they had chosen for the new garden, to see if the two of us thought it was a good idea. This was just a ruse, a power play. She knew it, Dr. Cook knew it, and we knew it. But we were tickled to be part of her manipulations. And we would get a personal tour of the arboretum by its distinguished director.

We arrived early for our meeting with Dr. Cook and took a little stroll down one of the arboretum paths. In less than five minutes Charles exclaimed, "Honeybun, what is this fabulous tree?"

I had no idea. I'd never seen anything like it. Its enormous pale green oblong leaves were arranged in whorls so that its canopy was a gorgeous kaleidoscopic pattern of shifting sunlight and shadowed foliage.

The tree was labeled MAGNOLIA 'SILVER PARASOL', a fitting name, because looking up into it was indeed like looking at so many parasols opened against the sun. We asked Dr. Cook about the tree. In the archives he found us a feature article in a 1954 *Arnoldia*, the arboretum's publication. It turned out to be a chance seedling, a cross between an American magnolia, *tripetala*, and a Korean magnolia, *hypoleuca*. Forensic botany had revealed that as a hybrid it took the best qualities of each of its parents. From the native American *tripetala*, it inherited a magnificent leaf structure and flower shape but not the *tripetala*'s shrubby growth and the foul smell of its flowers; from the Asian *hypoleuca*, it got its stately silhouette, sweet flower fragrance, and silvery bark.

Charles had to have one.

"Should I take some seeds?" he asked.

"It won't come true from seed," I told him. "It's a hybrid."

We searched magnolia nursery catalogues for 'Silver Parasol' without success.

Dr. Cook came to the rescue the next time he dined at the Carlyle with Mrs. Leventritt, amazing Charles by promising that the arboretum would graft a 'Silver Parasol' for us. Of course, this was really still a part of his wooing of Mrs. Leventritt. There was no reason on earth why the Arboretum should go to any trouble for us. But they wanted Mrs. Leventritt's three million dollars, and giving us a 'Silver Parasol' magnolia might help them get it.

A year passed. Then, one night, Charles called as usual when he got home after work. "Honeybun," he shouted happily, "guess what? Dr. Cook was in tonight to have dinner with Mrs. Leventritt, and he had good news! The grafts were successful. We're going to get our 'Silver Parasol'!" But that was followed by bad news at the next visit: All the grafts had died. This continued for two years. Again and again there were successful grafts that did not live a whole season. The tree was proving to be very difficult to propagate. Probably the arboretum would have given up except that Mrs. Leventritt kept asking Dr. Cook, "What's happening with Charles's tree?"

The ground was broken for the new M. Victor and Frances Leventritt Garden for vines and shrubs, terraces were laid out, planting was begun. Charles and I, each without admitting it to the other, gave up on ever getting a 'Silver Parasol'.

Mrs. Leventritt died in December 2004, after a short, terrible illness. At her funeral, a nine-by-twelve, black-and-white glossy photograph of her as a young woman, from her glamorous showgirl days, was propped on her casket. This was the first time I saw how extravagantly beautiful she had been.

Dr. Cook was there, of course.

"Good news!" he said to us privately, after we had paid our respects. "There are *two* healthy little 'Silver Parasol' magnolias waiting for you at the arboretum. Just let us know when you want to come and pick them up."

The Harvard horticulturists had discovered that the tree was more easily propagated by rooted cuttings than by grafting. They had produced eight healthy baby trees at the arboretum, all grown from cuttings.

In May, when it was safe to plant out a small tree, we drove up to Boston to collect ours. The young trees were each about ten inches tall, with a cluster of new bright green leaves. We were allowed to choose which two we wanted. We packed them carefully into a small cardboard box and brought them home, feeling, I imagine, the way adoptive parents do bringing their new child home: ecstatic, scared by our good fortune, filled with hope, worried we might do something wrong to kill the little things.

In our garden, Charles and I took photographs of each other holding the cardboard box with the two baby trees nestled inside. These photographs inspired several watercolors, one of which I included in my autobiography series.

We named the two trees Frances and Victor, for the Leventritts, and sited them with much consideration, Frances at the southwest corner of an open seating area, where she might eventually shade a cast-iron bench, and Victor across from her, where he would provide texture against the backdrop of woods. They'd be able to see each other every day across the garden. Each was positioned so that we would be able to look

The young trees were each about ten inches tall.

up into their stunning kaleidoscopic canopies, for that is the great beauty of this tree. I dug holes proportionately much larger to the size of the plant than any I'd ever dug before, and prepared the soil more carefully, screening our home-made compost through a sieve and mixing it with peat moss and humus. We made cages to keep out deer and rabbits and draped burlap over them to prevent sunburn.

That first summer, the little cuttings grew amazingly from ten inches to over five feet. We had to enlarge their cages every few weeks, and it was evident they did not need the burlap screening them from the sun. They thrived unlike any trees I had ever planted. That fall, we took photographs of each of us standing next to the trees to send to Dr. Cook and the horticultural staff at the arboretum. I stood next to Frances and Charles next to Victor, because Victor had grown about a foot taller and Dr. Cook knew how tall Charles was, so it would seem even more impressive.

The next summer, Frances and Victor each grew another six feet, both of them becoming taller than either of us. Charles pruned off Frances's lower branches to about five feet off the ground, to encourage more top growth.

"She'll grow even faster now," Charles said, "since she doesn't have to waste any energy down there at the bottom. Victor is okay the way he is, he's doing fine. In a year, we'll be able to stand under him."

That summer, the banana grove next to Frances got so enormous that it shaded out her west side, and she grew away from it and became lopsided. I could see how much this troubled Charles. I knew he understood I loved the banana grove, and that he did not want to ask me to remove it. But we had the other banana grove alongside the garage, after all, and our 'Silver Parasol' trees were two of only nine in the whole world. Frances must be protected at all costs and allowed to grow into her own shape, unhindered by common bananas. I decided to rip out the bananas.

"I'm sure Frances will recover next season," I assured Charles as he began digging out banana roots solid and heavy as cinder blocks.

"It's okay," he said. "Mrs. Leventritt was hunched over her walker, so it is only appropriate that this tree is going to be misshapen like she was."

With room to stretch her limbs, Frances began to fill out her west side.

"I like her this way," Charles told me. "Kind of twisted. She was like that."

In 2006, in preparation for my own colonoscopy, I went for a routine physical, my first in five years. When I sat opposite the doctor to get the results of my blood test, I knew something was wrong.

"Your PSA is quite high," he told me.

The PSA (prostate specific antigen) number is an indicator of possible prostate cancer. A healthy reading should be less than 1. Once the number rises above 4, there is some concern; 5 is worrisome.

"It is almost a hundred," the doctor told me. "You will need to get a biopsy to be certain, but with such a high reading, chances are you do have cancer."

I quelled my panic. Terrifying as the news was, my real concern was telling Charles. A PSA reading so high probably meant that the cancer might have been diagnosed earlier if I'd been going for regular checkups. I had never wanted to disappoint Charles. I had never wanted to bring any sadness into his life. My fear of doctors had resulted in this.

Charles was waiting in the apartment for me, for the

news. I tried to remain calm and optimistic, but I didn't succeed.

He didn't scold or criticize. He held me tight and said, "Honeybun, we'll get through this together."

Then we both cried in each other's arms. Charles's sobs were so deep and wrenching, I felt I needed to stop crying just so he would. But even as I went to wash my face and to compose myself, Charles's deep, heaving sobs continued. I had ruined everything. I went back to hold him again.

"I'm so sorry, Honeybun," he gasped between sobs. "I should have forced you to go for your checkups."

The day before going to the city for the biopsy, I was in Orient. It was a distractingly warm, sunny, blue March day spangled with early daffodils, like the March day on which I first took possession of my house in its empty field. I walked through the garden saying aloud to favorite trees and shrubs, "I do not have cancer.

"I do not have cancer," I said to the feathery evergreen nandina; to the prickly mahonia; to the rare trochodendron, bronzy with winter foliage, which I had grown from a tiny cutting mail-ordered from Heronswood. "I do not have cancer," I said to the two 'Silver Parasol' magnolias, already grown taller than Charles.

"I do not have cancer, I do not have cancer, I do not have cancer," I said to my hardy palm trees, to the bare rosebushes, to our weeping Alaska cedar atop which Dinger used to perch.

Four days after the biopsy I was in the city apartment, not in our garden, when the doctor called to say, "It is cancer."

Memorial Sloan-Kettering, where I would meet my oncologist—a word I had never expected to use regarding my own health—is down Second Avenue, within walking distance of our apartment. On the way to my first visit, Charles and I passed our usual neighborhood restaurants, where we had spent carefree evenings. They seemed alien now, as if they would never be the same again. Then we passed shops and restaurants just beyond our usual walks, ones I might never get to know. I decided that if I could get to each corner before the light turned red, it would all be a mistake and I would not have cancer. I was never fast enough. The flashing red hand stopped me at each corner. Then the sprightly little WALK! man, all outlined in white lights, urged me on. He seemed to be coming along with me. Did he have cancer, too? I wondered if everyone I passed on the street had a terrible medical secret.

There were so many florists on the way, all of them that day filled with orchids. Potted houseplants did not interest me the way garden plants did. Now I couldn't help noticing orchids. White, yellow, maroon, big corsage orchids or sprays of tiny spidery orchids. They all seemed cheerless, unreal, nothing like plants in our garden. Fake.

I thought, *If I am hospitalized, I hope no one brings me flowers. They will only remind me that I am not in my garden.*

Freddie and Sylvia and Karen were waiting at my doctor's office, along with Frieda's estranged husband, Adam, who had a long family history of cancer and would know the right questions to ask, or not to ask. We learned that day that the biopsy showed that the cancer was too advanced for either surgery or radiation, both methods usually successful in curing prostate cancer when it is found early enough. The cancer had spread beyond the prostate gland, as far as my lungs, so removal of the gland was of no use. The only therapy available to me was a hormone treatment. My oncologist, a tall, stunning young woman who managed to combine honesty with encouragement, explained this would not cure me of cancer. The goal was, in her words, "to put the cancer to sleep." Eventually the cancer cells might get smart enough to resist the treatment. My doctor said that in that case, she had "other things up her sleeve," rubbing her hands together gleefully in a way that I guessed was calculated to make me feel less terrified. And who knew? There might be other treatments available by then. New drugs were constantly in trials. The information came in a blur, but Charles and everyone else were taking notes.

The hormone therapy would reduce the testosterone my body normally produced; prostate cancer thrives on testosterone. There might be any number of possible side effects, all of which frightened me, but my doctor assured me they were not common. She reminded me I was otherwise healthy. I would have an injection every three months for the rest of my life, which I thought of as *until I die*. Edwin, who had much experience with medical problems, had advised me not to ask how long that might be. He explained that often when the doctor says, "You have three years," you die in three years. I decided not to ask.

I wanted to live to see my roses bloom. The diagnosis was in March, so it seemed reasonable to believe I would still be alive for the roses in June. But who knew for sure? What could I do beyond the hormone therapy to keep myself healthy? I asked my oncologist about a diet, perhaps foods to be avoided.

"Just enjoy yourself," she said.

I took that to mean, *in the time you have left*.

In the early days of the AIDS epidemic, when friends were dying horrible deaths, I got a case of the shingles, running down my forehead to my left eye. My doctor at that time was a gay man with mostly gay male patients. He sat me down in his office and looked at me sadly.

"Shingles are one of the most common indications of

being HIV positive," he said to me, as gently as possible but unable to hide the concern in his voice. "We'll give you a blood test today, and it will take about a week for the results, but I want you to start preparing yourself. You might consider a support group."

For the week, I had little hope of living much longer.

Freddie said, "In my bones, I feel you do not have AIDS."

The results came back negative. I just had shingles, nothing more, probably stress-related.

"Your blood is squeaky-clean," my doctor announced. "Marry me!"

Now I began wondering why no one called to tell me this cancer scare was all a big mistake. Someone else's charts. A misreading of the numbers. A practical joke to put me in my place and teach me to appreciate what I've got. Teach me to go for checkups.

No one called with that news.

April arrived. I gardened. In the garden, I did not have cancer.

As a child in Riverdale in the 1950s, I could see from our backyard the second-floor rear deck of the DePaolas' house next door. The DePaolas' daughter, Nini, their only child, had cancer. When my mother spoke of this, she never said the word *cancer* out loud, but instead when she got to that word in a sentence she mouthed it silently. I wasn't sure if this was superstitiously to ward off the disease by not naming it, or if it was because cancer was a shameful embarrassment, like running off with a married man, which also might not be spoken aloud. Either way, the effect was to make me worry obsessively about ever getting cancer myself. I didn't want to be whispered about behind my back.

Nini DePaola never left her house, but I sometimes saw her leaning against the railing of her sun deck, wrapped in a housecoat patterned with big pink and purple 1950s flowers. She was pale—ashen, really. Her hair was lank and her eyes glassy inside brown circles. She was older than I was, maybe in her late teens or early twenties when I was seven or eight. Every now and then my mother told me that Mrs. DePaola said Nini would like me to visit her, that it would bring her some enjoyment just talking to me. But I was afraid to go there. I wasn't afraid of Nini but of her unspeakable illness. My mother never forced me to visit Nini, so I only knew her as a pale figure leaning over the railing of her high deck, alone against the sky, staring ahead at nothing, like the figurehead of a doomed ship.

Nini jumped off that second-story deck one day in a suicide attempt. I don't remember if she died then, or if she died of cancer later on. After Nini died, the DePaolas sold the house and moved away.

When I was diagnosed with prostate cancer, my reaction was to keep it a secret. But that was a fleeting impulse, gone in a second. I needed my friends' love and support.

I had to spend more time in the city, seeing doctors. I resented being taken away from my garden. Even a day away might mean missing some blossom I had looked forward to since winter. Each time I came into the city, I brought huge bouquets of daffodils for Charles, flowers that might bloom and fade before we were both in Orient again to see them. After years of bringing cut flowers from the garden into the city on the bus for my mother, I was now using Charles's double-container method to get them safely through the trip without spilling water or breaking stems.

One day, as I was cutting daffodils for Charles, a tiny male ruby-throated hummingbird landed on the ground right at my feet, its iridescent feathers catching the sun. It seemed much too early in the season for hummingbirds, and this one was even smaller than usual, half the size Dinger had been. Its heart was beating so rapidly I was worried for it. I yearned to touch it, to cradle it in my hand, but I did not want to frighten it.

I got down on my hands and knees. The tiny bird's pinpoint black eyes did not show fear, but its heartbeats made its whole body tremble.

I thought of the hummingbirds that had come to say farewell to Charles's mother. I wondered if this was a sign that I did not have long to live. But the tiny bird's presence was soothing, not disturbing. Maybe it was Evelyn, I mused, come to comfort me. I put my face close to its own and spoke to it for what seemed a long time.

"You are so beautiful," I told it. "Thank you for letting me stay here next to you."

I was relying on a team of real doctors now. There could be no harm in asking the hummingbird to grant me a magical wish. I put my lips as close to the gentle creature as I dared without frightening it, and I whispered, "Help me to have many more years with Charles."

It flew away, low, over the garden, through the new spring foliage.

Love-in-the-Mist

I stopped working at the nursery when I turned sixty-two, to concentrate on my health. I wanted to spend whatever time I had in our garden.

"Now that you can be at home full-time, let's get a dog," Charles decided.

"That's a huge investment in time." I was thinking about my illness. The dog would probably live longer than I would. I didn't say that to Charles.

"We have the time."

I had read that having a dog often extended a person's life. Research has definitely proven that having a dog can help to keep blood pressure at a safe level. I wondered if Charles was thinking about my health, or if he really wanted a dog.

Snowball popped into my mind.

We would have to get a small dog that we could take with us on the bus back and forth to the city. Our co-op rules permitted one dog per apartment, up to fifteen pounds. We debated rescuing a dog from a shelter versus selecting a purebred puppy from a reputable breeder and decided that we wanted to train a young puppy. At our ages, and because of my health, we needed a dog that would be well behaved and did not have issues. We considered many small breeds. Charles suggested terriers, particularly a West Highland White or a Cairn, but all terriers are diggers and there was the garden to think about. I had often thought about having a Schipperke, because I had once heard that they were the longest-lived of all small dogs, sometimes living to twenty-two (although, since my diagnosis, this now seemed irrelevant). Charles had had a toy fox terrier when he was a child. I had had two sweet miniature poodles when I was growing up, first Bamboo, when I was a child, and then Massimo, when I was a teenager. I loved them both dearly. When Massimo died, I was so distraught I decided I never wanted to have a dog again.

But now I wanted a dog like Snowball.

When Charles's mother passed away, his sister Angel had taken Snowball to live with her and her husband and their three dogs in Providence. We'd been up to visit a few times, and each time I saw her I loved Snowball as much as ever, her scruffiness, her sweet nature. But she was an odd little mutt. How would we ever find a dog like her?

One day, Angel called to report that while she was walking Snowball, a woman stopped her and exclaimed, "Oh, you've got a Havanese!" Angel had never heard of the breed, nor had we. Charles did some research online, and found that indeed there was a breed of adorable small dog that had originated in Cuba but almost went extinct during the revolution. They had been the pets of the aristocracy, and when the rich Cubans fled to Florida and South America, many left their dogs behind in the care of household help, believing they'd be returning soon. Over the years, most of the dogs in Cuba perished. But a dog lover in Colorado, Dorothy Goodale, bought eleven dogs from Cuban refugees and started to breed them.

"Honeybun, we *can* find a dog like Snowball!" Charles gushed, happy to make me happy.

Charles began researching Havanese breeders online. We wanted a breeder near enough that we could visit. Also, we did not want to have a puppy flown from somewhere far away, because we thought that would be too traumatic for it.

"Here's a breeder in Greenwich, Connecticut," Charles said, calling me to the computer screen. "Her dogs are beautiful!"

The breeder was Claudia DeVita, and her kennel was called DeVita Havanese. We scanned through her website, oohing and aahing at puppies, learning the terminology of their colorings: white, champagne, pied, black, black-and-white, silver. Some were all one color; some were white with one black circle around an eye; some were white splotched with black patches; some were black with white eyebrows, chest, and paws.

"That's the one I want!"

"No, that one!"

"What's wrong with this one? Why don't you like it?"

Charles worked carefully on an introductory e-mail letter, to make it as evocative as his ad in the Personals that had gotten us together. He talked about our Orient home and garden, our city "pied-à-terre," how we were both middle-aged and had had dogs when we were growing up but had waited all these years, until we felt we could provide the kind of home a dog needed.

"Tell her I'm retired now and can spend full-time nurturing the puppy. It won't have to be alone at all ever, or spend any time in day care, or have to have a dog walker."

"And we should point out that he'll have a country house near gorgeous beaches for him to run on."

Claudia DeVita responded quickly, saying that she got hundreds of letters a year, and that Charles's was the best she'd ever read. She would work with us. There was a litter due in a few months. She would send photos as soon as they were born.

"We're going to have a puppy!" Charles shouted. "Do I know how to write a letter?"

"You write the best letters!"

"Well, you edited it for me. And now we've got to prepare for getting us a puppy."

Charles ordered all the books he could find about the care and training of Havanese. We read them in tandem, each of us with a different book, reading passages aloud and discussing every instruction.

"They all make it clear this is a breed that is going to need daily grooming," Charles warned.

"But Snowball doesn't look like she's been groomed all that much."

"If we're going to get one," Charles said, "we're going to take care of its coat. That is the real glory of this breed. They're called 'The Silk Dogs of Cuba,' after all."

"We can do that," I answered, not knowing what I was talking about. My childhood poodles had always gone to groomers, too matted and tangled by then for us to do anything about their coats. I leafed through the "Grooming Your Havanese" instructions in one book, about a dozen pages. "It will just take practice," I said, trying to sound confident.

While Charles read aloud the complicated grooming procedure, I flipped through the pages of my book looking at cute puppies.

The most important thing we learned was that Havanese needed early and careful socialization to prevent them from being shy or, worse, snappy. One book even suggested that as soon as the new puppy came home, its owners should give a party for a hundred people: tall people, short people, white people, black people, fat people, skinny people, people with beards, people with funny ties, people with big hats. That sounded like fun!

The puppies were born on February 22, 2007. Their mother was Shimmer, a lovely champagne-colored dog; the father was Polar, pure white. Both were champions. There were seven puppies, four champagne-colored and three black with white eyebrows, chests, and paws. Claudia e-mailed a photo of them, all gathered up in her arms like an overflowing cornucopia. One little black-and-white face in particular tugged at my heart.

When the puppies were six weeks old, Charles and I and Karen drove to Greenwich to see them. As we walked into the kennel, the seven puppies were suckling their mother. We had read that it was important to meet the mother dog, to see how she behaved, because it would be she who would educate the puppies in their first weeks. Shimmer was gentle, entirely comfortable and welcoming when I placed my hand into her cage, and the little black-and-white puppy that I had loved in the photos, a boy, let go of his mother's teat and waddled over to gently nibble my finger.

"This is the one!" I said.

We were allowed to play with the puppies on a blanket for a while. My favorite, the one I had chosen—in fact, the one that had chosen me—was the most energetic and inquisitive, a tiny, shiny black-and-white bundle of fur no bigger than Charles's hand, squiggling this way and that over the squirming knot of his siblings. He especially took to Karen, licking her face and ear incessantly. I hated to go home without him.

Claudia told us that she would call us when she thought the puppy was ready to leave his mother.

"It might be at nine weeks, it might be at twelve. I'll know when it is time."

The next few weeks seemed endless. There was already a place in my heart devoted to the little ball of black-and-white fur, and it ached from the separation. We acquired a crate, dog beds, a carrying case, a leash, combs, brushes, water bowls, food bowls. We puppy-proofed the house and the apartment, following the instructions in various books. We enclosed the garden with wire deer fencing stretched on metal stakes, and stapled the bottom edge to the ground. Any gap or hole under the house or the shed was sealed with wire mesh.

"It says here that lilies are poisonous to dogs," Charles said, reading from yet another list of instructions.

"I'm not digging up my lilies."

'Sheherazade', an Orientpet lily, a cross between Oriental and Trumpet types, was one of the glories of the garden, a few original bulbs that had now spread into huge clumps of seven-foot-tall stalks sporting hundreds of maroon-and-white flowers. I looked forward to them every summer.

"We don't have to," Charles said, to pacify me. "I don't think he'll eat them, anyway."

We still had not settled on a name. We had at first thought we'd be getting a female dog and had decided to call her Rosie. I was so enamored of that name that Charles tried to convince me that it could be a male name too. I didn't think so.

"When I was a little boy I always thought if I got a dog I would name him Rover," Charles confessed.

"Then that's his name!"

"But it doesn't sound very Cuban," Charles offered, without much conviction.

"It doesn't matter. He was born in Greenwich, Connecticut. He can have a quintessential American name!"

When Rover was nine and a half weeks old, Claudia called to tell us he was ready to leave his mother.

"I always thought if I got a dog I would name him Rover."

Charles and I drove from Orient to Port Jefferson, an hour west, and took the ferry from there to Bridgeport, Connecticut, a misty hour-long crossing on Long Island Sound. Then we drove down to Greenwich, another hour.

Rover, already grown quite a bit, was romping happily in a playpen. I imagined he was glad to see us, but I knew he was just naturally happy.

"He's a little goofy," Claudia told us.

"Perfect!" Charles said. "We are, too."

"Now, you can name him whatever you want, but he has to have an official AKC name for his registration, and I have a theme name for each of my litters. This one has to have the words *in the* in it, like Walk in the Park, or Man in the Moon.

"How about Catcher in the Rye?" I suggested, but that didn't go over too well. "Okay, then, how about Love-in-the-Mist? Because that is one of my favorite flowers, *Nigella*, and also because it was misty on the Sound this morning."

"Love it!" Claudia said.

So Rover became, officially, DeVita's Love-in-the-Mist.

Charles later pointed out that *Nigella* is actually Love-in-*a*-Mist, not *th*e-Mist.

"I don't care. Rover is going to be Rover."

We put him in the carrying case we had brought, in which I had put a T-shirt that I had slept in so that he would get used to my scent, and I held that on my lap in the car and sang silly songs to him as we drove back to Bridgeport, songs my mother sang to me when I was a child. When we boarded the ferry the foghorns blasted, but Rover was calm and relaxed on my lap, studying everyone and everything with great interest. I pointed out the sights to him as if I were talking to a child. He seemed to like having my hand resting on him. He was comfortable on the ferry crossing, and snoozed on the drive from Port Jefferson to Orient.

"He's not looking back," Charles said. "I don't think he's missing his mother or his brothers and sisters at all."

"He's looking forward to his new life. Aren't you, Rover?"

"Goodbye, kennel. Hello, Orient!"

As we drove, I decided that my goal was to raise Rover to be a good host and a good guest, a charming little dog that would be welcome anywhere. More than being a "daddy" to Rover, I wanted to be his Auntie Mame. I wanted to open his eyes to new experiences every day, and help him to be everything he had it in him to be. I began singing to him Mame's first-act song to her nephew, Little Patrick, the words about opening a new window and a new door, urging Rover to have a new adventure every day, to dance to his own rhythm, and not be afraid of being unconventional. To live life to the fullest.

I knew that I was on the right track when a few weeks later Rover was invited to an elegant outdoor summer party under a festive tent, where, when I asked his hostess for some water for him, she brought it in a martini glass. He sipped comfortably from the rim as I held it.

"What, no olive?" someone commented in passing.

"He likes it very dry," I answered.

Our routine was for me to keep Rover in Orient all week, while Charles was at work, and then Charles would come join us for his two days off. Puppy training happened while Charles was away; fun and games happened when Charles returned. Rover spent all week longing for Charles. It became obvious that Rover loved me, but adored Charles. Rover also was thrilled whenever Karen visited. He probably decided on our very first visit to Greenwich that we three were his pack.

One of my tasks was to wean Rover of separation anxiety. Like all puppies, he cried bitterly as soon as he feared he was alone. We had read that we must not go to him, no matter how heart-wrenching his pleas. Instead, we must wait until he was quiet, and only then go to him and praise him, so that he associated being quiet with getting what he wanted and was not being rewarded for wailing. Since I spent most of the days working in the garden, I set up a fenced playpen area in a sunny clearing and shaded it with a sheet. As long as I was in sight, Rover played happily and quietly, keeping an eye on me. The second I turned a corner, he began shrieking so hysterically I was afraid the neighbors might think we were torturing him on a rack. I couldn't let him wander freely to follow me because he was still small enough for a hawk to snatch him. In fact, one day a raccoon—which must have been rabid, since it was wandering about in daylight—came stalking Rover and got within three feet before I saw it. I snatched Rover up in my arms and yelled at the raccoon, and it fled.

"We can't ever leave him alone in the garden," I told Charles after that. "It's too dangerous out there."

"You're turning into Helen," Charles warned. I began to understand my mother's protectiveness of me.

I could let Rover out of the pen while I hung laundry in the sunny clearing. All the activity and the laundry flapping would discourage birds of prey, and he liked to play tug-of-war with the wet towels.

"Rover, you want to help hang laundry?" I'd call, and he'd come scampering out through the screen porch with me and follow along the seaweed path, nipping at my cuffs.

He'd settle down in the shade to watch me, alert for any sock that I might drop.

Line drying has always been one of my special pleasures. As a child spending my weekends with my aunts in their Washington Heights apartment, I used to go up to the roof of the building with my aunt Pennie to hang laundry. We would ride up the old elevator with heavy baskets of wet laundry, climb a few dark stairs to a thick metal door, and then emerge on the open roof. It was a strange terrain, a patchwork of black asphalt shapes edged in shiny tar, sloping slightly for runoff. Heat radiated in visible waves from the asphalt, like desert mirages, and when the tar got hot, it shone with oily rainbow colors. When we collected the laundry, the feel of sun-dried fabrics, stiff and rough, was so unlike the soft, fluffy laundry that came out of a dryer, and the smell was as fresh as daylight.

I loved those laundry days, the old-fashionedness of it, the idea we were doing something the way it had been done for hundreds of years.

When I bought my house, it was wired for only fifteen amps of electricity. It had never contained a telephone, television, dishwasher, clothes washer, or dryer. I was not going to beat my laundry against the rocks on the Sound beach. I would need a washing machine. But I would have no dryer. I intended to line-dry my clothes.

As soon as I moved in, when the garden was still only an open flat field, I stretched a fifty-foot clothesline diagonally east to west to catch the most sun. I anchored one end to a locust post that had a bird feeder on top and the other to the side of the garage. I cherished my laundry mornings, any day bright enough for drying. I loved the feel of damp fabric as I clipped it into place, the differing textures of terry cloth and cotton and linen, the fresh-washed wet smell, the glaring brightness of morning sun on white T-shirts and the shadow-puppet patterns of my hands clothespinning shirt shoulders into place. I loved the sound of the smart flaps of sheets in the wind, the trapeze artist postures that long-sleeved shirts froze into in winter, the hot sun-baked smell when the laundry was collected. For twenty-odd years, I never felt the lack of a dryer. Once in a while, on the most humid days of August, clothes might not dry, and then I'd hang them in the house. In winter, laundry might freeze as I hung it, flannel sheets transforming to expanses of sparkling ice crystals, stinging my fingers, but the sun soon thawed the fabric and dried it by early afternoon. I savored the difference between the smell of winter-dried laundry, almost sunburnt, and summer-dried, fragrant from the garden. Carrying in laundry on a blustery March day was like bringing sunshine into the house.

As the garden matured around my clothesline, less and less of the line remained in enough sunlight to be usable. A lilac 'Superba' swallowed up the locust post where the line was attached, and next to it the rugosa 'Rosarie de l'Hay' reached out six feet in all directions, so the first twelve feet or so of the line became engulfed in thorny shrubbery. At the garage end, a Virginia magnolia eventually sent up a whole colony of trunks. Over the years, the last twenty feet of the line disappeared into the magnolia's canopy.

My clothesline had become to me as much a garden feature as any of the trees and shrubs. I ordered sheets and pillowcases in bright colors—turquoise, hot pink, electric orange—because I liked the way those colors looked on the line. They cheered me, especially in winter. They made me think of sun-bleached North African souks where freshly dyed cloth is hung to dry. The year we met, Charles took stunning photographs of this colorful laundry against a backdrop of flowers and foliage, then, in winter, vividly silhouetted against snow. He also took some of my favorite portraits of me, hanging laundry, which became the basis for watercolors. But I could hang only a small load on the diminished sunny stretch of line, and it was also becoming harder for me to undo the line and store it out of sight when I wanted the garden to look its best for visitors. Charles did not like the clothesline, especially if it was still up when visitors arrived unexpectedly. He never exactly said so, but he always answered, "No," when I asked him if he had anything he needed washed. He took his own laundry back to the city with him. I tried to do my drying during the week, while he was in the city, and have the line neatly hidden before he returned. But the weather didn't always cooperate.

Edwin suggested an Italian-designed, collapsible clothes-drying rack, made by Brabantia, with sixty meters of line amazingly incorporated into its structure.

"It opens up like a big umbrella," he explained, "and easily folds for storage into its own zip-up case."

I ordered one, and after one use, I couldn't imagine how I had managed without it for over twenty years. Charles called the design superb. "Those Italians . . . ," he said. We got rid of the unsightly clothesline.

Rover loves the fluctuating patterns of shade cast by the drying sheets and towels as they flutter from the Brabantia. On a hot day, he settles down in one patch of shade, and then moves to another as the sun traverses overhead, always keeping an eye out for any dropped laundry.

Rover knows the garden intimately—the paths, the shortcuts through the plantings, the gate at which to greet visitors. Once in a while, his long hair snags on a rosebush, and then he knows not to struggle but to call us with a pathetic whimper. He waits patiently while we untie his hair from the thorns. Once, a particularly onerous seedpod released hundreds of sticky seeds into the hair on his right ear, where they stuck like Velcro. It took me several hours to untangle each seed. I didn't mind the time. I was not going to cut off his beautiful hair.

Charles began photographing Rover on the day we brought him home—cuddled inside my shirt, curled up asleep in his donut bed, a tiny puppy stretching up to examine daffodils. I took a picture of the two of them asleep on our porch swing, Charles on his back, Rover on Charles's chest, sprawled on his back, his little black-and-white legs and arms splayed out every which way, both snoring gently. As Rover grew up, Charles's portraits became more dramatic. A favorite is of Rover sitting under a huge *Petasites* leaf, which, because of the scale and because no one expects a leaf to be so enormous, makes Rover look like a three-inch-tall dog.

Our sunny open clearing is now only just wide enough to contain the new drying rack. The borders of trees and shrubs all around have grown tall and thick, which is just as well, because there are swimming pools in the yards on both sides of us now. From the clearing, I can no longer see Charles walk down our shady path on the other side of the *Clethra barbinervis*. The dense foliage creates a *giardino segreto*, secluded from the world around it.

Our seating area is in what's left of our shrinking sunny clearing. We inherited three ornate and very heavy cast-iron garden chairs from Mrs. Leventritt. I painted them a vivid yellow-green called "chili pepper" and arranged them in a semicircle under the passionflower vines, where Frances, the 'Silver Parasol' magnolia, now appropriately shades them. We found neon hot pink cushions for the chairs. In high summer, pots of pink and magenta zinnias cluster between the chairs, along with turquoise-flowered tweedia and sky blue plumbago. We keep creating new pictures by moving containers of bright annuals to wherever color is wanting. Gladiolas, hibiscus, nasturtiums, cleome, and of course always a container of love-in-a-mist—each in their season has its place.

In this seating area, I've tried to capture the slightly decaying elegance of an overgrown old Italian garden. I used to long without hope for the little wall lizards that dart among the grotesqueries of Villa d'Este to complete the picture, like the lizards I'd first seen in Bermuda. I've now learned that these lizards have colonized parts of Long Island, having escaped decades ago from some pet-shop shipment. I had no idea they could survive our winters. Our next project is to pave the sunny clearing with random bluestones. The stones will become warmed by the sun, perfect for lizards to scurry across. We'll border the patio with a low dry-stone wall to provide a safe habitat for the tiny creatures. Then we'll introduce them into the garden.

Rover will love chasing them across the stones.

A Cucumber Magnolia and a Pink Horse Chestnut

In a garden, time thrusts upwards with peony shoots, outwards in all directions with the leaves of a mimosa, unfolds with the bursting of a rose. Time repeats in endless cycles of growth and death, patterns full of surprise and beauty, no matter how fleeting. The future is sun after rain, no more than that and all of that. A zinnia seed sprouts quickly if the weather is hot, and blooms soon in sunshine. A magnolia may take seven summers to bloom. A gardener waits. The waiting is all.

When I was a child, a summer day seemed a whole year long. No matter how many ways I found to entertain myself, from mornings bicycling to evenings chasing fireflies in our Riverdale backyard, there always seemed to be more time left to fill. Now my days go by so quickly, and my list of chores is so long, I can't find enough time.

The butter-knife blades of daffodil foliage burst through March's muddy black earth, followed by a flower stalk flaunting its wrapped parcel of buds. The wrapping falls off, a jaunty round flower basks in spring sunshine, fades, then the foliage collapses like road kill. Does this take a long time? Or is it over quickly?

It depends on what else is happening in the gardener's life.

My first cancer treatments were spaced three months apart, hormone injections to lower my testosterone. Before that, three months had seemed like not a very long time to me, a summer soon gone, but after the worrisome first days and weeks following the diagnosis, a stretch of three months without having to be at the clinic became a delicious eternity, an entire summer to be spent in our garden. By that first fall, my PSA was down from close to 100 to below 1, at .85, perfectly normal for a healthy man my age.

I became optimistic. I would garden. I repeated to myself a phrase I remembered from Beverley Nichols's writings: "Time is kindest to a gardener, for it gives more than it takes."

But the regimen of medications stopped working that winter. The PSA climbed. My doctor tried other medications. I had to be at the clinic every three weeks, and suddenly three weeks, once no time at all, became a luxuriously long time between treatments. Then, when one more new medication stopped working and yet another was tried, I had to be at the clinic every week, and now a few days off struck me as a long time. Eventually I participated in a clinical trial, for which I had to be at the clinic all day long for several days in a row, week after week, blood tests every half hour with EKGs tucked in between, so now one day off seemed a long time—not long enough to return to our garden, yet a stretch of time to be cherished.

I no longer trusted the measuring of time in standard units. Time had morphed into a multifaceted, palpitating, unfamiliar entity, continually reconfiguring, sometimes welcoming, often frightening.

Charles and I had been together ten years when I was diagnosed. To me it seemed like a minute and it seemed as if it had been forever, as if there had never been a time before Charles.

Now it seemed there would be a time for Charles without me. But Charles remained optimistic.

"I have never seen anyone as focused as you on getting well," Charles said.

"I want to live to see Frances and Victor bloom."

I began to picture my remaining time in relation to the trees that Charles and I planted.

Alongside our driveway is a stately cucumber magnolia. Taller than the house, it is the first thing a visitor to our garden sees. Charles grew it from seed, which he collected from a tree in Maine a few years before we met.

"It was in the fall. I saw this incredible tree in a front yard in Wiscasset," he told me when we were getting to know each other, one of the first of his stories I heard. "The whole tree looked like it was decorated with flaming red candles. Those were the seedpods. It was superb! I collected a lot of seeds, but only one seed germinated. A friend in Ithaca has it growing in his garden. I've never had a garden of my own to plant it in."

"Now you do," I said.

Charles's expression, like sun through a cloud, made me realize how important it was for him to feel that the garden was his, too.

His friend drove the magnolia down from Ithaca one stormy weekend just before our first Thanksgiving, cut back to fit in his car. Charles was dismayed about that, I could tell, but he didn't say anything. We struggled in a fierce nor'easter to get the tree into the ground, wind and sleet and branches slapping our faces. The sapling was four years old then, about five feet tall. After Charles's friend left, I broke open an aloe leaf and rubbed the juice on the wounds where the young tree's branches and leader had been cut off. The tree survived. The next spring, Charles pruned it to have one strong new leader.

A few months later, when we were visiting friends in Maine, we drove to Wiscasset, where, after cruising up and down unfamiliar streets, Charles found the original parent tree to show me. It was enormous.

"It will eventually tower over our house," I said that day, trying to picture it. Fourteen years later, it seems it has been here forever.

When I bought the house, there were two old apple trees where we had now planted Charles's tree. Their trunks and twiggy branches were spotted powdery gray-green with lichens. I cherished those trees because they reminded me of the mossy ancient trees I had loved in English woods, trees beneath which Druids might have assembled, or past which Elizabeth I might have strolled on her way to meet Essex.

Soon after settling in, I planted the climbing musk rose *Rosa moschata plena* next to one of the apple trees and 'New Dawn' next to the other. Both roses prospered, sending up long canes through the old trees' branches, then cascading down from the canopies. *Rosa moschata plena*'s white flowers in large sprays bloomed right after the apple trees, like a second flush of apple blossoms, wafting their honey fragrance in every direction, even far down the lane. 'New Dawn' draped its tree in swags of shell-pink irregular flowers. This rose— its form and color and fragrance—always reminds me of the roses in 1930s movies that covered the walls of romantic country getaways, black-and-white roses whose color and fragrance my imagination supplied, and which, for all I know, might have been fake props.

These apple trees filled with roses were seen by anyone passing along Village Lane. The trees hadn't been pruned or sprayed or tended in any way for some time before I bought the house, but their apples were delicious, although I imagine smaller than they might have been if the trees were healthy.

I don't know the variety—dark red like 'Delicious', but rounder and with a crisper tang. In late summer they fell by the hundreds beneath the trees. My neighbor Mona told me that Stosh Soito had always let her gather as many as she wanted for applesauce, and I told her to continue to take all she could use. She made applesauce for me from time to time, pink from the red skins and overly sweet from too much added sugar. I'd pick up an apple to eat now and then while I gardened, biting around the worms or blemishes, but most of them I'd toss into the garden beds to become compost.

The first summer I spent in my house, a doe and her fawn found the fallen apples and started coming back every morning at the same time. I watched from a downstairs window, enthralled. I felt so lucky to be here, in this three-hundred-year-old house, starting a new garden, and watching this epitome of a bucolic scene through panes of wavy antique glass.

The old apple trees eventually began to drop diseased and dead branches. I discovered rot inside the trunks. I wasn't interested in spraying with chemicals, or any other heroic measures to keep the trees alive. I wanted them to die naturally, as gracefully as possible. When they reached the ends of their long lives, first one and then the other, I had them cut down and put out of their misery.

The roses that had climbed up into them were by then mature enough to stand on their own as large mounding shrubs. 'New Dawn' covered about a hundred square feet, with a companionable 'Madame Alfred Carriere' intertwined in its branches. *Rosa moschata plena* had clambered over a 'Dawn' viburnum into the winter honeysuckle.

But the garden along the driveway seemed incomplete without a tree until we planted Charles's cucumber magnolia. In summer, its profuse large yellow-green leaves now block our upstairs view of the Civil War obelisk and of the Button-wood Tree. In winter, its bare up-facing branches create an elegant structure, an obelisk itself, and through the lacework of twigs I can see the Monument again, and because the leaves are off the Buttonwood Tree, I can glimpse Edwin's house.

A few yards further along the driveway is our pink-flowering horse chestnut 'Fort McNair', shamelessly sexy in spring with erect flowers like triple-scoop cones of raspberry sorbet. Charles had long admired a pair of spectacular pink-flowering horse chestnut trees in Central Park, near the Conservatory Water, where children sail toy boats. He took me to see them one spring. Their flowers were a particularly delicious pale champagne pink.

"This is what I want for our garden," he said.

The trees were not identified by any plaque, so we would have to either wait until we saw the exact color in a nursery or go by catalogue descriptions. On a drive through Massachusetts, not at the right season for horse chestnut bloom, we stopped at Sylvan Nursery to inquire about various cultivars with flowers in shades of pink. In their catalogue we found a description of 'O'Neil's Red' that sounded like the tree we wanted. Our car was not big enough for us to take one with us, so we ordered one for delivery.

"As long as we're getting one, why not get two?" Charles said. "You know Mark will want one if we have one." Mark was Steve's partner, the Steve who had brought over the Personals page with Charles's ad. He was landscaping their new large property in Orient and often looked to our garden for inspiration.

Sylvan delivered the trees, Mark collected his from our driveway, and we planted ours. The next spring it bloomed *white*. The trees had been mislabeled. Sylvan replaced them free of charge with two trees clearly labeled 'O'Neil's Red'.

We gave one to Mark, who happily kept his white one, too, because it did have particularly beautiful foliage, if not pink flowers.

We dug up ours that had bloomed white and gave it to another friend. The hole was there, ready for our new tree. But while the tree was still standing in its burlap-wrapped root ball in our driveway, we saw an 'O'Neil's Red' blooming in a local nursery. The color was a harsh red very different from the lovely pink flowers in Central Park. Charles hated it. We gave that tree to yet another friend.

"We can't go on replacing horse chestnuts every year," I said to Charles.

"Why not, if we don't like the color? Grandmother Essie always said to be particular."

"Well, at least let's wait until next spring so we can see the trees in bloom at the nursery before we buy another one."

The following spring, three years after beginning the search, we did find the tree we wanted at a nearby nursery, where we were able to select a beautifully shaped 'Fort Mc-Nair' from their growing fields.

Six years later, it has grown tall enough for me to stand under. Eventually it will shade the driveway and almost touch our cucumber magnolia. Anyone turning down Village Lane in spring will be presented with its pink flourish, in full bloom in time for Charles's May 17 birthday. I have planted the rose 'Climbing Pinkie' at its base, so that in June the tree will be a waterfall of pink roses. In autumn, passersby will see the flaming red candles of Charles's cucumber magnolia. November through March, the pink pom-poms of our 'Dawn' viburnum will show over the hedge. The entrance to our garden will be a beacon in every season.

Throughout Orient, there are magnificent old trees, generations old, centuries old, that Charles and I point out to each other whenever we drive past, as if they were old friends we've unexpectedly come upon after many years. Sometimes we make a detour just to see how a favorite tree is doing. *How is the willow at the end of Village Lane? . . . If they don't water that snowball tree, they are going to lose it! . . . The copper beech looks like it's suffering in this drought!* It's a little like my aunts' commentaries on the strangers passing in front of their Washington Heights apartment windows when I was a child.

About a half hour west of us, slightly hidden from the main road, there used to be a mature southern magnolia that had survived many northeastern winters. Its glossy dark foliage and dinner-plate-sized white flowers recalled Charles's native Georgia. Charles always found this tree easily, although when I looked for it on my own I couldn't remember where it was. We checked on it each spring.

It looks like it made it! . . . Yes, but it looks awful. Most of it is half-dead. If it doesn't leaf out soon, it might not make it through another winter.

Then, after one severe winter, we saw it blackened from windburn and sunburn, a skeleton holding on to a few curled, parched leaves. We never found it again. We still mention it, sadly: *Remember that huge southern magnolia?*

Every once in a while, a hurricane uproots one of these old trees, or batters it irreparably. The feeling of loss is devastating. During Hurricane Bob, in 1991, I was in the city, checking on the storm by phone with Edwin, who was in his Orient house, when he exclaimed, "There was just a tremendous crash! Hang on!" He left me dangling, I heard him exclaim loudly in the background, then he returned to the phone.

"Skip, I think the Buttonwood Tree just came down!"

It was like a kick to my stomach.

It turned out that it was only one major limb that had broken off, but a limb that was wider in girth than many other trees' trunks, and that for generations had stretched out a sheltering bough over the Main Road.

That storm brought trees down all over Orient, followed by a flurry of handmade signs saying, THANKS A LOT, BOB!

Here and there, some old trees are dying untended, slowly, of old age and disease, or from repeated droughts. New property owners have had old trees cut down, either because they shaded a garden too much or because they were too close to the house and might cause damage in a storm. I would probably let the house go first. When I say that to Charles, he doesn't believe I mean it. He is more sensible, but still he is outraged when a lovely old tree is taken down just for convenience.

"They should be shot for doing that," he says.

We were faced with possibly losing a tree ourselves when our new neighbors to the south put in a swimming pool. They needed a safety fence around their entire property and discovered that my deer fence along our shared property line veered four feet onto their land for a few yards near the woods. In this narrow pie-shaped wedge was our rare and beloved Chinese fig hazel, *Sycopsis sinensis*. It would have to be moved. I got the news in August in the midst of a heat wave and drought, the wrong time to move an established tree.

The fig hazel was dear to me. Its small leathery leaves remained green even during the most severe winters, never curling the way rhododendrons and some other broad-leafed evergreens do. All winter long, the bright green tree promised summer. I loved it so much that I had once tried to order a second one from the same southern New Jersey nursery from which I had gotten it. It turned out that they no longer carried *Sycopsis sinensis* because it hadn't proven hardy for them.

"Well, mine has survived seven winters here for me," I told them, with a hubris that I now regretted, faced with up-rooting it.

The fig hazel was by then about fifteen feet tall. Moving it and getting it to survive at any time of year would have been a challenge; a transplant during a drought seemed likely a death knell. I knew if anybody could move this tree success-fully, it was my friend Oswaldo, a young man from Guate-mala who had once worked at the nursery with me.

The day before the scheduled move, the weather broke. It rained a whole day, a steady, gentle rain, and the next day was cool and bright. As I hovered nearby and worried him and cautioned him and advised him, Oswaldo moved the fig hazel just four feet, to within the actual line of our property, where, suddenly, it looked like it was always meant to be, pro-viding shade for an evergreen Florida star anise.

I dragged a hose to it and soaked its roots until the ground was muddied. I hosed it top to bottom every hour. The next day, it rained again, and was ten degrees cooler. I continued to drench the foliage several times a day as the weather cooled with more frequent rains. Still, I knew it would not be until the following spring that I could be sure the tree had survived its move. *Would I be there to see?*

"This is a clethra Barney Nervous," I overheard Charles ex-citedly telling visitors about our *Clethra barbinervis* during a fund-raising garden tour arranged by the Oysterponds His-torical Society. Our garden had become a regular feature of the annual event. He didn't get the name exactly right be-cause of his slight dyslexia, and this made me smile. I liked his version better.

Anyone could hear Charles's love for this tree in his voice.

Our garden became a regular feature of the annual event.

"It's related to the common summersweet clethra, but it's so different," he went on. "It has four seasons of interest. In spring when it first leafs out, it looks as if there is a chartreuse tulip at the tip of each branch, like a whole tree full of chartreuse tulips. Then, in early summer, it sends out sprays of flower buds that turn into little white bells dangling along the stalks. They look like lily-of-the-valley flowers. They bloom slowly, through midsummer, and then begin to turn into seedpods, little green balls hanging all along the stalks. Those stay on the tree through the fall, when the leaves turn vivid orange and purple. And then in winter, see, look," and here he took the group around to the path from where the trunk could easily be seen, "the bark exfoliates, so you have this fantastic gray and tan trunk with long strips of bark hanging off as if it had been shredded. It's a fabulous tree. You should have one!"

The clethra has after a dozen years attained the stature of a small tree, tall enough now to hide Charles from me. But I could picture his face as he went on about the tree's virtues.

A little later, I heard him calling our *Styrax obassia* a "jade-ball tree."

"That's what you said it was," he complained when I corrected him, privately.

"Yes, that *is* what I call it," I said, "because the seedpods look like chains of jade balls, but that's not what it *is*."

"Well, now everybody thinks it is," he said.

The trees Charles and I planted together, and the ones I planted before I met Charles, keep redefining the garden as they mature. They will be the backbone, and the garden will take shape around them. Here and there a sapling of a new, unusual tree pokes up through a bed of perennials, only a few feet taller. It will shade those plants someday, and they will stop blooming. We'll have to rethink the beds under those trees, choosing shade-loving groundcovers, and that will be that.

Our mimosa 'Summer Chocolate', a rare treasure, now shades beds of daffodils, peonies, iris, and roses. They are all suffering, except the daffodils, because they bloom early and the mimosa is one of the last trees to leaf out. It is not truly a mimosa, which is a tropical tree, but an *Albizzia julibrissin*, commonly called "mimosa" in the Northeast. We first saw this tree in Seattle in 2001, in the sales gardens of Heronswood Nursery, when Charles and I were attending the Garden Writers Association award ceremony. In an isolated area, I noticed a slender young tree with foliage of a color I had never before seen in nature, a velvety bluish maroon with warmer Chianti highlights. That one young tree seduced me immediately. At first, no one we asked knew what this tree was. Finally someone identified it, and then we recognized that it looked exactly like the familiar pink pom-pom mimosas that seed themselves freely, except for its stunning leaf color. But there was none for sale, and it seemed there might never be, no matter how Charles persisted or who he pestered with his inquiries.

Is that the only one in the whole world? I wondered. Our shopping cart full of rare little plants in tiny containers, so exciting a minute before, had lost its thrill.

"Don't worry, Honeybun, we'll get you one somehow," Charles assured me.

When a few minutes later I was attracted to a tree with large leaves the size and texture of rubber-plant foliage, bisected by beet-red stems, Charles urged, "Let's get one of those!" to take my mind off the 'Summer Chocolate'. It was a willow, *Salix magnifica*, but it looked nothing like any willow I'd ever seen, with its big shiny foliage, looming above felty-leafed Asian rhododendrons like a prehistoric tree in a natural history diorama.

The specimens for sale were all tall saplings.

"We can't bring something that big back on the plane with us," I said, pouting.

"Sure we can. We might never have the opportunity to find one again."

Charles added a three-foot *Salix magnifica* sapling to our full shopping cart. I felt better already.

At the airport, Charles checked his carry-on with our luggage and instead carried the willow onto the plane, nestling it between his knees for the seven-hour flight, his long legs already cramped by the seat in front.

"We should never have gotten it," I said, feeling bad for him. "Let me take it."

"No, Honeybun, you need your legroom, and I know how much you wanted this tree."

All that fall and winter, I felt the lack of the 'Summer Chocolate'. I asked our friends Dennis and Bill, who run the renowned tropical nursery Landcraft Environments, to let me know if they came upon a source for one.

The next spring they called to say they were bringing over a surprise for me.

"We know how much you wanted one of these," Dennis said, handing me a 'Summer Chocolate' sapling, not yet leafed out.

I was overwhelmed. And a little scared that I might kill it. But now, eight years later, the tree with its amazing foliage has become one of our garden stars.

Another "not-for-sale" tree that I coveted was a variegated Kousa dogwood at VerDerBer's Landscape Nursery in Aquebogue, forty minutes west of Orient. It poured the day we visited, but we wandered around in the rain anyway. Along one side path we came across six young saplings with strikingly colorful foliage, gold-centered with dark green borders. I had seen variegated Kousas in catalogues, but none with this bright coloration. We found the proprietor and dragged him over to show him the tree we wanted, but he told us he was growing them for future sale and would not sell us one. We were getting drenched, so I didn't think it was worth pursuing. I climbed back into our car to sit, wet and disappointed. Charles did not follow me. I watched the rain cascade down the windshield for half an hour. Suddenly, Charles was knocking on the passenger window. Behind him was the proprietor, carrying the best specimen of the Kousas, freshly dug, he and Charles and the little tree all dripping wet. They loaded it into the backseat.

Charles switched on the ignition, beaming. "Honeybun, I got us a variegated dogwood!" As we drove home, he told me how he badgered the nursery owner and dropped the names of horticultural acquaintances until the poor guy finally relented and dug up the tree. It is hard to say no to Charles, even in a deluge.

Another rarity, our monkey puzzle tree, a Chilean native, has survived a dozen winters. Charles and I had discovered a mature monkey puzzle tree on Shelter Island, between the North Fork and the South Fork, along Route 114, and whenever we drove past we always pulled over to the shoulder to get a good look. Once we knew the tree was hardy here, we planted a twelve-inch sapling in our garden. This peculiar conifer, *Araucaria araucaria*, has razor-sharp scales instead of needles, arranged along each tubular branch like the armor of a pangolin. It got its common name supposedly because it is so prickly that monkeys can't figure out how to climb it. Although it has been hardy for us, it is slow-growing this far north and will take many years to be tall enough for me to stand under. In the meantime, we give its blade-armed branches a wide berth when we are gardening in its vicinity.

Nearby is a dwarf sweet gum, a variety called 'Gumball'. It has developed into a ten-foot rounded mass of twiggy branches, unlike most of our less formal trees and shrubs.

"It looks like a huge cannonball that wasn't invited to the garden party but came anyway" is how Charles sees it.

Charles took over the training of a weeping spruce that I had coaxed to about six feet tall. This tree would lie prostrate on the ground, snaking its branches this way and that, if it were not staked up a vertical support. I'd gotten it up as high as I could, using broom handles lashed together. Charles, with a tall A-frame ladder and his height and long arms, was able to train it up another ten feet. It now cascades in waves of velvety needles alongside the much taller weeping Alaska cedar, like a sidekick.

We started a *Cryptomeria dacrioides* from a four-inch Heronswood cutting. I had been coveting a *Dacridium* I had seen in photographs, a New Zealand conifer that looks a bit like a Norfolk Island pine, but that tree would not survive on Long Island. Then, when I discovered the *Cryptomeria dacrioides* in the Heronswood catalogue, the name suggested it might look like a *Dacridium* but be hardy. I decided to try it. Starting a tree from a tiny cutting is always a gamble, not just because of the challenge of keeping it alive, or because of the many years needed to grow it to any size, but because after all those years it may not turn out to be something you even like. This one is a keeper.

One season it sent out a twisted branch too close to the leader. I came upon Charles just as he was about to prune it off.

"Stop!" I yelled.

"It's going to strangle the leader and take over," he warned.

I begged him to let me train it away rather than cut it off. He was unconvinced by the elaborate structure that I jerry-rigged out of bamboo stakes and ties made from torn bedsheets. But after two seasons, when the framework was removed, the branch behaved in a well-mannered way.

We keep adding trees: a longleaf pine, a bigleaf magnolia, a 'Venus' Kousa dogwood with huge white flowers, a yellow-tipped Oriental spruce, a blue-tinged *Sequoiadendron*. Planting a tree embodies boundless optimism. After my diagnosis, it became for me a shamanistic ritual: I must live to see the tree grow to maturity.

One night, I dreamed that I was in the garden setting out sturdy new plants, each in a black plastic container. Out of one container, along with the bright green foliage, a rainbow surged, its stripes of color moist and tingling against my fingers as it arced high into the sky and descended somewhere far away. Wherever I carried that pot, my end of the rainbow came along. I understood that I could set it down anyplace I wanted and it would stay.

It was not a pot of gold at the end of my rainbow but a new tree.

"I wonder what people will say about our cucumber magnolia a hundred years from now," Charles mused. We were sitting on the cast-iron bench under Frances, her parasol foliage patterning us with fluctuating light and shadow, almost as if from a stained-glass window. Rover was sleeping in the dappled shade at our feet.

"And the red horse chestnuts we've spread around all over Orient," I reminded Charles. "And Frances and Victor!" I looked up into Frances's shimmering canopy.

"All our trees. Will they wonder what sort of crazies lived here, to have planted so many rare trees on a third of an acre?"

That set me wondering about what will happen to the garden when it is no longer ours. Even if Charles and I both make it to a healthy old age and live to see our trees attain maturity, at some point the property will have a new owner. Maybe someone who wants a sunny lawn. Who does not want to rake leaves. Who worries that a tree limb might crash into the roof. What will become of Frances and Victor?

I had been so excited to find Mr. Soito's peonies growing happily on my property that March day in 1983. They were a continuum from an earlier garden, cherished by an earlier gardener. I built my new garden around them. Will the next gardener cherish the plants I have loved and nourished? Will he or she feel reverence for my seaweed path alongside the banana grove, mulched with eelgrass I lugged from the beach in plastic trash bags, trip after trip, year after year? There is no reason to believe the banana trees will mean anything special to a new gardener, and eelgrass has almost died out along our shores, so the path cannot be rejuvenated as it decomposes. Will anyone else care about the passionflower vines or the little palm tree I grew from seed? What about Charles's cucumber magnolia, standing guard at the entrance to our garden?

There is so little room left here for a new gardener to express herself or himself. I had been presented with the whole empty field around that clump of peonies. The next gardener may want to remove rather than add, to make her or his mark.

When I first moved here, I heard an old-timer say, "The trouble with you new people is, you come here and buy property and you think you own it." At the time, I thought it was a rude remark. But I came to understand that we are all simply caretakers of these homes and gardens. Someone will follow us, for her or his own little while.

If I die first, will Charles keep the property? I once promised I would outlive him, to spare him the pain of grieving, but that was before my diagnosis. If Charles dies first, would I be able to maintain the garden by myself? Should I find a new home for Frances and Victor right now, before they have grown too large to be moved?

On Village Lane, friends and neighbors have died or moved away. New neighbors, decades younger, come to visit the garden. They do not know that our house is the Soito house, or that our 'Festiva Maxima' peonies are Mr. Soito's peonies. Fewer and fewer people know that anymore. That kind of information is disappearing along with the old-timers. It saddens me.

These new visitors, some of them gardeners already, some of them not yet, ask the usual questions about our garden, but I find it takes me longer and longer to dredge up the names of our plants. Not just the Latin names—that wouldn't be too disturbing; but sometimes a common name eludes me for hours. The names of some roses I have forgotten completely, and there is no way to ever find out, as I did not always keep records. We have over fifty varieties of hosta, but the ones whose names I still know can be counted on my fingers. Charles often calls across the garden for me to identify a particular tree or shrub or perennial for a visitor. I am relieved when I can.

Every spring, Edwin asks me to come over to his garden to point out which plants are weeds and which are not. His garden is almost all shade now. The trees I helped him plant when he first bought the property now tower over it. One time he asked me to remind him of the name of some little plants with sky-blue flowers that were coming up here and there in his woodland garden.

"They come back every year," he told me, "and I know their name like I know the back of my hand. But for the life of me, I cannot remember what they're called."

"Edwin," I answered, "those are forget-me-nots."

Asters and Goldenrod

October days are like the farewell performances of a cele-brated soprano: Some days are as glorious as any at the height of summer, even more glorious because they remind us of our mortality. Death is all around us on such unexpectedly warm, sunny days under blue skies peppered with swallows. Annuals are giving up, tomatoes have stopped ripening, the stubbly remains of perennials are bleached to straw. There are a few roses, special because they are scarce. Purple asters glow alongside bright goldenrod, but the purple of asters is not a youthful color, and not a happy one. It has a sadness about it that comes from maturity and a beauty that comes from tran-sience. The asters will not last much longer. A passing shadow turns them violet, just for a moment. The garden, exposed and vulnerable to whatever lies ahead, soaks up the warm sun, believing it can sing forever. Being optimistic and ro-mantic, I pretend to forget what's coming.

It's easy to forget, because the October garden glows as if a fine spun-gold veil is draped in swags from the highest branches. Slanting rays color the air into a presence as tan-gible as the last flowers. Lighting designers use a gel this color to flatter divas, to take off decades. The October garden is blowsy and disheveled and makes mistakes, but the amber spotlight is more forgiving than the unrelenting July sun. There's mildew on the zinnia leaves. I don't look too closely.

Monarchs hovering on the buddleia are a copper cloud trembling against purple, the colors of a Spanish shawl. How can these papery creatures fly all the way to Mexico? They seem incapable of flying to the next flower, wobbling erratically now this way, now that, winding up somewhere they may not have intended. A hummingbird is in their midst, jewel-like and riveting, another improbable voyager. I want them to stay here in my garden. Stay, and hold summer here in a cage of copper and emerald.

The passionflowers have stopped blooming, leaving behind so much greenness, such masses of vine and tendril and leafage, overwhelming reminders of their reach for the sky. Once the flowers have gone, I can't recall the scent of their perfume even though I can remember its power. And I remember the bees on them—so many. How they must have loved that perfume!

The nasturtiums go on as well, summery as ever. I know—as they seem not to know—that one morning soon I will find them melted, soft as braised lettuce. The caladiums have already fallen, ambushed.

These warm fall days are yesterdays, the way it was last month and before that the way it was in July. And before that, the way it was when I was a child.

After a day's work getting the garden ready for winter, Charles and I walk down to the beach. It basks in summer-like warmth. Pebbles glow chalky white until the clear water polishes them, colors them to bright pinks, ambers, shiny black. Any one of them might be a keepsake pendant. The water is mirror-glassy yards out to where bluefish-hunted minnows velvet the surface. A cormorant pops up from nowhere like a jack-in-the-box.

We swim.

Pebbles glow chalky white until the clear water polishes them.

•

When the days have finally cooled off, I get around to the chores that the heat and humidity of summer kept me from facing. We must coordinate bringing indoors the tender tropicals in their massive containers before a frost kills them, and yet try to keep them outside as long as possible while they are happily growing. Some will die at fifty degrees, some can take a frost. Each plant must be washed down, pruned, weeded, and checked for insects. Then we have to make space for it in the house.

I bring fewer and fewer plants inside each fall, partly to leave enough room for the two of us to get around, partly because it has become harder for us to lift the heavy containers.

"This is the last summer for 'Purity'," I say. "I'm not going to bring it inside." The hibiscus, now five feet tall, has flamboyant white flowers with long, protruding magenta stamens that look like Fourth of July sparklers. I know Charles would be glad to be rid of it. It takes up an entire corner of the kitchen.

For a few years, Charles and I kept alive a Red Abyssinian banana, *Ensete maurelii*, digging it up before the frost came, chopping off its enormous red-and-chartreuse leaves, and storing it all winter like a piece of lumber propped up in a corner of the kitchen, its huge leek-like root stuffed into a plastic garbage bag. In the spring, back in the earth again, it would quickly unfurl its brightly striped and splotched leaves with lacquer-red midribs, brilliant when backlit by the morning sun. We named it Amonasro, after Aida's father, king of the Ethiopians in Verdi's opera. It thrived over the years, its trunk reaching the girth of a telephone pole. We needed help to carry it inside each fall, and out again when the days were warm enough, in a sling made from an old bedsheet.

One summer, some garden demon—raccoon, deer, opos-

sum, we never discovered what—took a disliking to Amonasro
and began attacking it at night. In the morning, we'd find the
huge leaves shredded, the vivid red midribs broken off close to
the trunk, the trunk itself deeply gouged and bleeding sap. The
damage was catastrophic and inexplicable. Why would this
plant so enrage a wild animal? We tried protecting Amonasro
with a cage of deer netting, but the unseen enemy was unstop-
pable. Amonasro eventually wound up on the compost heap.

My *Jasminium tortuousum*, another tender plant in a container, revealed to me an unexpected willpower so stunning
that I will always keep it. *Tortuousum* is a vigorous vining jasmine, easier to grow than most, blooming continually but not
profusely, with slightly fragrant, star-shaped white flowers.
One fall, I had cut it back severely and placed it in a west-
facing living room window with plenty of warm afternoon
sunshine to keep it happy. While all the other plants in those
west windows stretched toward the light, pressing against
the windowpanes like schoolkids watching a snowfall, the
jasmine began sending an exploratory vine in the opposite
direction, out into the room: a six-inch slender green shoot
when I first noticed it but soon twice as long and aiming
straight up toward the center of the living room. I didn't understand why it was turning away from the sunlight. I was
going to weave it back into the jumble of its other branches,
but I was intrigued. I let it do what it wanted, and watched.
Day by day it stretched, without support, up into the room—
three feet, four feet. The vine, slender but sturdy, continued
at a steep angle, straight as an arrow on a determined journey,
until it was almost touching the brass four-armed chandelier.
One morning, I saw that it had wrapped its slender growing
tip around the nearest arm of the chandelier.

I realized then what it had in mind: It had intended all
along to grab hold of the fixture. From the window, it had

grown ten feet away in a direct line, never veering off course even a few inches, never collapsing under its own weight. The jasmine was determined to reach the chandelier at all costs. But how did it *know* that the chandelier was there?

When the tender tropicals have been brought inside, the hardy ones that will overwinter outdoors must be protected. The Basjoo bananas can survive outdoors with no protection. They die to the ground like peonies, to send out new shoots when the ground warms. But if they are given winter protection, they will grow more rapidly in the spring, and I always want that dramatic surge of giant foliage, so I designed what I call a "banana cabana," constructed out of two-inch-thick Styrofoam insulation panels to house the clumps. The Styrofoam, unfortunately, is powder blue. This structure gets covered with a clear plastic drop cloth to allow warming sunlight in but keep out rain, which might rot the banana stalks. Burlap strapped on over the plastic with silver electrical tape shades just enough to prevent winter sunburn. It is not an attractive construction.

"Don't you think the banana cabana looks like an installation by Christo?" I ask Charles. I know he thinks it is an eyesore.

My *Trachycarpus fortunei*, the windmill palm, the largest of my hardy palm trees and my favorite, met a sad end. This palm was grown by Plant Delights Nursery from seed gathered from a wild stand of the palms in North Carolina. It was the palm that always reminded me of my childhood Florida vacations. It survived five winters and reached a height of six feet, but one winter, in damp weather after a bad freeze, the central growing tip rotted, leaving a hollow trunk filled with water.

I was devastated.

"Call Dennis," Charles suggested when I telephoned him

in the city, catching him before he left for work. "He'll know what to do."

This was Dennis of Landcraft Environments, who had given us the mimosa 'Summer Chocolate'. He advised me to cut the stump back until I found viable white pith, and then protect it from further rainfall. By the time I cut it back to living tissue, the trunk was only a foot tall. No rain was predicted, so I left it uncovered.

"We've saved the palm!" I told Charles when he called after work that night.

The next morning, I went first thing to check on the palm. There was nothing left of the new white pith except a bunch of crumbs scattered on the ground around the stump. My heart sank.

I called Charles right away, knowing I would wake him. "Some animal ate what was left of the palm down to the core," I bemoaned.

"Hearts of palm!" Charles explained drowsily. "It's a delicacy."

Raking leaves is not one of our fall chores, since we no longer have any lawn. I let the leaves decompose where they fall in the beds, to return the same nutrients to the soil that they took for their growth, as would happen on a forest floor. The top layer of our soil has become loamy and black, filled with worm castings. I never liked raking leaves, anyway, even as a child in Riverdale, although in those days we were allowed to burn the piles of leaves and I did like the smell of the smoke. Once, years ago, when there was still a lawn here in Orient, a friend up visiting from Florida in autumn went to buy a second suitcase and raked all the colorful fallen maple leaves into it. She carted them home to spread over her suburban Miami lawn, under her key lime tree, to remind her of New England autumns. After that, I always looked at my fallen leaves with a connoisseur's eye. The neighbors' Norway maple leaves that blow into our garden don't decompose quickly. Those, and the leaves from the two 'Silver Parasol' magnolias, Frances and Victor, huge and tough as a giant's flip-flops, get dumped on our compost heap.

As November turns into December, visitors to the garden often ask, "Aren't you sad that everything is dying?"

"Not dying," I correct adamantly, "going dormant."

I point out daffodil shoots and bright rosettes at the bases of sedums, promises of spring. I think of December as a beginning, not an ending.

The spring catalogues arrive in December—Brent and Becky's Bulbs, Fairweather Gardens, Plant Delights—my winter reading. Nestled into an arm of our couch, I fill out long order forms while Charles, in his armchair between the flamboyant red leaves of our philodendron 'Prince of Orange' and the dangerously prickly arms of a variegated agave, reads the newest *Art in America*. Rover is flat on his tummy at Charles's feet, like a miniature bear rug, his nose between his paws pointing at Charles, waiting for an invitation to play.

"In a minute, Rover," Charles says. Rover looks up, hopeful. "Let me finish this article."

Rover sighs, comes to me, and curls up at my feet, giving me a quick worried glance. He knows I am not well, and is very concerned.

"And don't disturb Skippy!" Charles says. "He's ordering a hundred new plants."

We both know I won't order a tenth of the plants on my list. The fun is in picturing how each of these plants would look in the garden; imagining their slow or rapid growth; fantasizing about future visitors to the garden who will exclaim ecstatically over yet one more rare plant. Imagining the garden next year. Imagining us both in it.

This past summer had been the most magnificent ever in

our garden, as if the garden had decided it would put on a spectacular display. We got plenty of rain in the spring, and mild days, and it was clear that all the Orient gardens were going to be lush. I figured that was why things were looking especially wonderful. But I soon realized it was more than that. Our trees and shrubs, mature now, presented themselves as clamorously as debutantes dressed in their most tasteful gowns, graceful in their extravagant new foliage, some adorned with spring flowers. At their feet, perennials and ground covers intermingled, choking out weeds. Variegated Solomon's seal wove around hostas and astilbes, creating an undulating surface of contrasting textures and leaf shapes; epimediums surged along the ground like a gentle green tide amid violets and creeping comfrey, the foliage on wiry stems shimmering on the sun-dappled surface.

But I was most overwhelmed by the stunning effects that our roses achieved. Because our trees have matured to the point of shading the garden almost completely, roses that are not thought of as climbers have reached high into trees to search for sun, draping themselves unexpectedly in sprays of color above our heads. 'Rugelda', a hybrid rugosa with peony-shaped butter-yellow flowers tinged with raspberry, not a climber, got itself up into the lower branches of our *Styrax obassia*, and just as the tree's lily-of-the-valley-like flowers faded they were replaced by clusters of sunny roses. 'Double Plum', an early hybrid China, not a climber, stretched out of the shade at the base of a deodar cedar to drape itself over the conifer's needly branches with sprays of wine-colored pom-poms. 'Dr. Huey', the rootstock graft of a rose long since gone, decorated our variegated Kousa dogwood with its dark red single blooms alongside the dogwood's white flowers. 'Awakening', the double sport of 'New Dawn', reached every which way across and through tall blueberry bushes, the Chinese fig hazel, the 'Eskimo Sunset' maple, and into a massive tangle of roses, orange 'Westerland' and violet 'Weilchenblau'. The species *Rosa glauca* hugged every limb of a tall mimosa, anchored by an ivy-like vine that I do not know the name of, starring the tree with single pink flowers.

The roses that are climbers, and were planned to give these effects, outdid themselves, creating storybook pictures. 'Madame Alfred Carriere' sprawled further in every direction than ever before, covering herself with fragrant ivory blossoms. 'Darlow's Enigma' tumbled down from high atop the winter honeysuckle, its bunches of small white flowers perfuming the garden for yards all around. 'Blairi #2', that earliest of pink climbing hybrids, with delightfully simple and disheveled blossoms, comfortably nestled high among witch hazels and European spindle trees. *Rosa moschata plena*, once climbing into an old apple tree long since gone, burst into a sheet of fragrance atop a 'Dawn' viburnum and the winter honeysuckle.

Everywhere I turned, I saw a garden picture as lovely as any illustration in a childhood storybook, each more evocative than any I might have hoped for.

And I wondered, *Is the garden doing this for me because this will be my last summer?*

I immediately replaced the thought with a determination to see the garden again next year, even more lovely than now.

The seasons have passed so quickly, and the years, too.

Freddie and Sylvia have been together thirty-two years. Rover's "aunt" Freddie and "aunt" Sylvia each turned seventy-five this year. Charles and I drive down Village Lane and out Orchard Street to their house now, instead of walking.

Martile has retired from singing. She has founded an opera company in Colorado Springs, Opera Theatre of the Rockies, which she has kept operating in the black for ten years. She teaches forty students a week. *Classical Singer* magazine named her Teacher of the Year in 2006.

Edwin spends half the year in Cape Town, South Africa, with his partner, Tim, who is not permitted to remain in this country longer than six months even though they are legally married, because of our immigration policies. They come to Orient in January and must leave in June. Edwin hasn't seen his summer garden since they met. Rover tugs on his leash to visit "Uncle" Edwin and "Uncle" Tim behind the Buttonwood Tree whenever we walk past on our way to the beach, even when they are far away in South Africa.

Charles's collection of American abstract expressionist prints has become renowned. The exhibition at our local Oysterponds Historical Society led to a lavishly illustrated article in *Architectural Digest*, and that in turn led to exhibitions around the country: at Haverford College; at the Knoxville Museum of Art; at the Cummer Museum in Jacksonville, Florida; at the International Print Center New York; and at the Pollock-Krasner House in Springs, on the South Fork of Long Island. In 2009, the Library of Congress acquired the entire collection.

Art Sites gallery in Riverhead mounted an exhibition of my autobiographical watercolor series. There were more than one hundred watercolors by then, and the story they told included scenes from Charles's childhood, painted from his old family photographs, snapshots that paralleled moments from my own childhood. The paintings were hung in chronological order, in a line wrapping around nine walls, narrating Charles's and my lives from childhood through our meeting and onward to creating our garden. Amazingly, since Art Sites is in a small town, far from other galleries, *Art in America* reviewed my show.

In Charles's Seventy-ninth Street tree-pit woodland gardens, the climbing hydrangeas have made their ways up to the first crotches in the locust trees and graced the trunks for ten summers with their panicles of lacy flowers. But one night a neighborhood plant activist took it upon herself to rip the vines off the trees. She pulled the tallest vines down out of the branches, broke some of them off a few feet above the ground, even tried to uproot them.

"These vines are strangling the trees!" she yelled at our doorman, who tried to stop her.

Charles was devastated. He tied the stems she hadn't destroyed back against the trees and pruned off the ragged broken parts. One stem that was partially broken he mended with a splint and a bandage.

We put up signs laminated in clear plastic, one tied onto each tree trunk. They read: MADAME, YOUR ATTACKS AGAINST OUR HYDRANGEAS ARE VANDALISM. PLEASE STOP IT!

The woman sliced one of the signs in half.

A few days later, we got a call from a reporter from the *New York Post*, wanting to do a story about the "vine vandal." We were photographed in "tree-hugger" poses. The same day the article appeared, the television news channel NY1 featured the item on its morning broadcast. A week later, *The New York Times* picked up on the *Post* article.

"It's nice that there are other news stories besides murders and rapes and bombings," Charles commented to the *Times* reporter.

But the best interpretation came from a blogger: "The REAL story here is that these guys are growing CLIMBING HYDRANGEAS in a New York City *tree pit*!"

Frances and Victor are twenty feet tall after only five years. I did not expect flowers yet because I thought magnolias had to be at least seven years old before they bloomed, but when they had been in the ground for only three years I was telling their story to visitors, and glancing up, I saw huge torpedo-shaped green buds jutting from the ends of a dozen branches, each encircled by its whorl of parasol foliage.

I gasped aloud, "They're going to bloom!"

I called Charles in the city. "Guess what? Frances and Victor have buds!"

"You're kidding!"

"I hope, if they open, the flowers will last until you get here."

"They'd better!"

That weekend, Charles and I watched the buds day by day. Each bud started off smooth and bluish green, tinged with maroon. Then the guard petals folded back revealing a long, pure-white pointed bud, brandished from the tip of its branch as confidently as an epée. During the course of the day, each white bud unfurled, its narrow, slightly crinkled petals drawing back into an enormous fourteen-inch-wide pure-white flower. At the center was a concoction that could have been created by a confectionary chef, a ring of frosty white filaments from which protruded a magenta spire of tiny little curls, like a marzipan scepter for the Queen in *Alice's Adventures in Wonderland*.

The flowers emitted a fragrance unlike any other in the garden. Every single visitor who climbed a ladder to smell a flower—and many came just for that experience—exclaimed exactly the same words: *Oh, wow!* The fragrance was compared, inconclusively, to peach, banana, pineapple, watermelon, vanilla, and even bubble gum.

Rover has made friends up and down Village Lane, and visits them for playdates, always wanting to stop at his "aunt" Karen's house along the way. He rides the bus with us back and forth to Manhattan. He has traveled with us to Spain, where we visited Madrid, Córdoba, Seville, and Granada. While Charles and I looked up from our guidebooks at Moorish arches, Rover did his own sightseeing, nose to the ground. I liked to think he was judging how long ago Ferdinand and Isabella had proceeded in pomp down that cobbled street.

The summer of 2009, he came along to Venice, where Charles photographed him sitting on Attila's throne on Torcello. That same year, Rover was chosen to represent the Havanese breed on *Dogs 101* on Animal Planet.

He's happy in the city, checking out who's been at the tree pits recently, but he adores our Orient garden. He's interested in everything we do there, never letting us out of his sight, sometimes watching from the shade as we dig and prune, sometimes digging with us, getting his nose muddy.

I have returned the old clothespins to the faded turquoise woven basket in which I found them the first day I walked into this house in March 1983. Dear old weather-worn friends, sturdy, reliable, dependable, they have stood me well these almost thirty years. They have outlasted the lightweight wooden ones that spring apart on their first use and the flimsy plastic ones that break when you snap them into place on the line, all made in China. But there were never enough of the old ones. I reserved them for the heaviest laundry that needed the firmest clasp. They're retired now. I had guessed they might be older than I was when I found them, and now they are almost a third of a century older. They're on the wooden sink in the mud porch, for the next owner of this house to discover. I hope they are treasured.

When I set them in their place, I looked long and lovingly at the mud porch, the wavy panes of glass looking out to our garden, the old woodwork with traces of the original milk paint, the wooden sink, the broad hand-hewn crosspieces holding the wooden storm door steady. How I love this house! Yes, it was my entrance to the garden, on which I poured most of my devotion, but I love this house, its crazy angles, sloping floors, mismatched doors and windows. What a privilege to have become part of its three-hundred-year-plus history.

House! I wish you well.

Now, this December, as Charles and I sit in our living room, cozy with our winter reading, Rover inches closer to Charles's toes, still hoping to play. He touches Charles's foot with his right paw.

"It's pretty amazing, don't you think," Charles says, looking up from his *Art in America*, "that when we get a dog, he winds up on national television. Rover, you're a star!"

Rover lifts his head, hearing his name.

"And pretty amazing that your collection winds up in the Library of Congress!"

"And that your illustrations for our book won the Garden Globe! And your watercolor autobiography got a fabulous review in *Art in America*!"

"Keep going!"

"And we have two specimens of the rarest magnolia in the world!"

"I hope I am here to see Frances and Victor bloom again." I immediately regret having turned the conversation to my illness.

But Charles says confidently, "You will be."

I recall a remark I heard once, somewhere: *Cancer is as devastating to the caregiver as it is to the patient.*

I am filled with love and gratitude and sadness, and awe, for this remarkable man.

I fold down a page of my Plant Delights catalogue. "There's a new red-leafed banana being offered." I am trying to sound optimistic.

"Where are you going to put that?" Charles asks, not looking up from his magazine.

"I guess you're right. We don't need it."

"No! Get it!" he urges enthusiastically. "Put it in front of the woods."

The Screened Porch

Charles and I are sitting at the glass-top table on our shady screened porch, watching a flock of small white butterflies, dozens of them tossed in the breeze like confetti, bright in sunlight against the faded lilac of Verbena bonariensis. *Now they hover closely in a fluttering white swarm, now they fly off in all directions as if blown apart. Then, by chance or deliberately—it's hard to say—they are back in a huddle, and on and on. Neither Charles nor I has ever seen this dance of the white butterflies before, and we are entranced. This moment: these tiny bits of white tossed this way and that by fate, or defying it; Charles's rapt attention; his profile in shadow against sun-drenched salvias and verbenas; his lips parted in amazement; Rover curled sleeping at his feet—that will forever be the garden for me.*

Acknowledgments

I am indebted to Karen Braziller for inviting me to partici-
pate in her Red House Writers Workshop. This memoir went
through many transformations over almost ten years of work-
shops, nurtured by many readers along the way. I am grate-
ful to Joyce Beckenstein, Cynthia Beer, Edwin Blesch, Karen
Braziller, Maureen Cullinane, Charles Dean, Lucille Field
Goodman, Amy Gross, Faye Hirsch, Stewart Johnson, Anne
MacKay, Paula Mauro, Valerie Scopaz, Nadezhda Shoken, Jane
Smith, Timothy Smulian, Manuela Soares, L. B. Thompson,
Amei Wallach, and Liz Welch for their careful reading of my
work and for their invaluable criticisms.

I want to express my gratitude to the Ludwig Vogelstein
Foundation for their two generous grants, which enabled me
to complete this project.